ADVANCE PRAISE

"In Hired to Quit, Inspired to Stay, Craig tells his inspiring story of building a culture that teaches happiness, gives back, and inspires people to live their own dreams while at the same time outlining real problems with real solutions."

—ROGER HAMILTON, FOUNDER OF ENTREPRENEURS INSTITUTE; CREATOR OF GENIUSU, WEALTH DYNAMICS, AND TALENT DYNAMICS; AND AUTHOR OF *NEW YORK TIMES* BEST SELLER *THE MILLIONAIRE MASTER PLAN*

"I've known Craig for a few years now, and he's come up with so many ideas to improve businesses. Anyone who has started a company or thought about it can benefit from Craig Handley's book. Look no further if you want to see firsthand how to scale a business and navigate cultural differences, as well as how to fail epically, conquer crisis, and restart a company on the brink of failure. He covers it all, with important reminders about the greater purpose of starting and running a business by building an amazing culture that teaches people how to be happy and how to dream."

—DAVE ASPREY, FOUNDER OF BULLETPROOF AND AUTHOR OF *NEW YORK TIMES* BEST SELLER *THE BULLETPROOF DIET* AND *HEADSTRONG*

"There are so many moments in the life of building a business that an individual will go through and so many leaders who don't share those challenges honestly. They don't like to talk about the restarts, the turnarounds, and all the times they've made mistakes, but Craig talks about those things openly and, more importantly, provides insight into how to handle those challenges. He also outlines a way to build a culture that trains people to be happy and encourages them to live their own dreams. In short, it's a great story."

—JJ VIRGIN, CNS, CHFS, FOUNDER OF MINDSHARE COLLABORATIVE

"The life of an entrepreneur is a roller coaster of emotion, financial ups and downs, big visions, and the sometimes hard realities that come with it. You get a ringside seat here."

—YANIK SILVER, AUTHOR OF *EVOLVED ENTERPRISE*

"Authentic, experienced, and funny, Craig Handley bares it all in his new book. He takes you from A to Z, begging you to ask hard questions, which will inevitably lead you to success. His writing style makes his book a valuable and relatable resource for all entrepreneurs looking to start or continue their journey to greatness personally and professionally."

—JOE MECHLINSKI, CEO OF SHIFT AND *NEW YORK TIMES* BEST-SELLING AUTHOR OF *GROW REGARDLESS*

"Raw, honest, real, and packed with actionable strategies, Hired to Quit, Inspired to Stay will share with you the roller-coaster journey of an entrepreneur and show some hard realities of running a business. If you are looking to build a powerful enterprise, listen to what Craig has to say in this book."

—AJIT NAWALKHA, CEO OF EVERCOACH MINDVALLEY

"Hired to Quit, Inspired to Stay should be required reading for anyone thinking of being an entrepreneur or working for an entrepreneur. This is the new roadmap for how to fail and succeed while navigating the complex matrix of the entrepreneurial mind."

—DORIAN DICKINSON, SERIAL ENTREPRENEUR AND MANAGING PARTNER OF GSD INNOVATIONS, LLC.

"Craig Handley is a living superhero (I met him in Haiti), but more importantly, he's the kind of guy I'll listen to, a guy I'll observe and emulate. Why? Because he's an executioner. Not only is he an idea guy, but he's a guy who closes the loop where so many others fall short. Yes, it might take setbacks and failures before it closes, but Craig closes it, and he shares it all here! Hired to Quit, Inspired to Stay is raw, authentic, and vulnerable and will indeed show you how to be an executioner too!"

—FRANK MCKINNEY, SIX-TIME BEST-SELLING AUTHOR, INCLUDING *THE OTHER THIEF*

"Hired to Quit, Inspired to Stay is a triumph of honesty. In dissecting pivotal moments of his entrepreneurial journey, Craig produces countless teachable moments in a way that only he can. What you'll enjoy most is the rawness and his willingness to show his mistakes. That is lacking these days. It will make people feel human. Craig makes me think of St. Peter in the Bible. He is a passionate nutball."

—STEVE SISLER, AUTHOR OF *THE FOUR PEOPLE TYPES AND WHAT DRIVES THEM*

"Craig Handley has written the handbook for creating a truly great company. Step by step, through failures and successes, Craig guides us along his journey with gut-level honesty, and in the process he teaches us the key factors that make a business great. If you're committed to your own and your company's success, Hired to Quit, Inspired to Stay has to be on your must-read list."

—CHRIS ATTWOOD, COAUTHOR OF THE *NEW YORK TIMES* BEST SELLERS *THE PASSION TEST* AND *YOUR HIDDEN RICHES*

"Most books in this genre are heavy on inspiration, but light on action. This book is different—it's a virtual 'cheat sheet' for persevering through the ultimate highs and lows of entrepreneurship. It's timeless while obviously based on real-life experience."

—MICHAEL LOVITCH, SERIAL ENTREPRENEUR AND COFOUNDER OF THE BABY BATHWATER INSTITUTE

"Hired to Quit, Inspired to Stay is a must-read for anyone who is serious about building an intuitive and winning culture. Craig has lived through all of the challenges and shares the secrets of building a great team and a wildly successful business! It is a MUST-read!"

—BILL WALSH CEO AND FOUNDER OF POWERTEAM INTERNATIONAL

"I've known Craig for more than fifteen years and personally witnessed his professional growth. He used to come to my office, and he would be constantly reinventing himself to create new value. Over the years I watched him evolve from a one-man show to a business selling over $150 million a year in products. He has constantly found new ways to remain relevant and restarts are something he's mastered and something every business needs to learn how to do. He's always cared about people, so learning how he has built an amazing culture to support his business goals is inspiring as well. This book is a great toolbox to help any business scratch and claw their way to success."

—KEVIN HARRINGTON, ORIGINAL SHARK ON *SHARK TANK* AND INVENTOR OF THE INFOMERCIAL

"Hired to Quit, Inspired to Stay takes you behind the scenes of a company on the brink of disaster to rolling in profits over and over again. It's a thrilling roller-coaster ride of key lessons learned from the entrepreneurial trenches. Craig's sage advice on business partnerships toward the end is pure gold."

—JIMMY SWEENEY, CEO OF HONESTEONLINE.COM

"Hired to Quit, Inspired to Stay is the kind of book you read with a pen and highlighter. It's rare to find a business book with such specific, actionable advice. Craig holds nothing back. The painstaking process that led to his company's vision, the actual financial numbers, the resources that helped him along the way—he covers it all in detail."

—JANET BRAY ATTWOOD, *NEW YORK TIMES* BEST-SELLING AUTHOR OF *THE PASSION TEST* AND *YOUR HIDDEN RICHES*

"Craig delivers valuable insights, and he shares well-thought-out information in this book. As an entrepreneur, he demonstrates the importance of knowing your numbers and how to plan for success in business. He clearly unveils clever ideas to implement right away, such as hiring for a culture fit and establishing core company values. This book is a must-read for entrepreneurs and business leaders to shorten their learning curve while sharing their passion with the world—plus it's brilliant and fun!"

—LEE RICHTER, AUTHOR OF *CREATING EVENTS TO REMEMBER* AND CEO OF GOASKLEE.COM

"As a woman entrepreneur (and at the risk of being politically incorrect), I admit I was skeptical that a 'man's man' like Craig could show us how to create success with heart. I had no doubt that he could give us a blueprint for creating a business organization with a winning bottom line, but success in business today demands being vulnerable, asking for help,

and listening to your intuition. Hired to Quit, Inspired to Stay beautifully addresses every one of these heart-based areas. Craig is a true visionary, and Hired to Quit, Inspired to Stay is the quintessential handbook for authentic success in these changing times."

—DEBRA PONEMAN, BEST-SELLING AUTHOR AND CEO AND FOUNDER OF YES TO SUCCESS SEMINARS

"I've seen a lot of business owners tackle the culture/engagement/ turnover problem, but Craig's approach has re-energized a tired space. He's managed to duplicate his enthusiasm and infuse it into his people, and his approach effortlessly translates in this book. You'll learn from his mistakes, but you'll be inspired by his recovery. His heart for his team pours through, and his vision sheds a bight light on how important it is to have fun at work. If you can't make it to ListenTrust to learn from Craig and have the best steak and queso fundido in the world, reading his book is definitely the best alternative!"

—KELLY CLEMENTS, FIRST FULL-TIME DREAM MANAGER

"Craig's book, Hired to Quit, Inspired to Stay, tells you about his tough journey and will inspire you to take that full bumpy ride to that bruising but successful finish. His unique style of truly focusing on his employees and having them use state-of-the-art technology, in a straightforward way with awesome training, of course is second to none! Having the willingness to understand failure will be a key lesson, along with remembering that values are like a compass; knowing who we are, who

we are not, and who we will be; and striving for that Dream Culture, with a focus on culture then talent—all, of course, while having fun along the way!"

—TOM ROCCA, KPI GROUP

"Craig is a big dreamer who encourages others to be the same! Through his honest, transparent book, he takes us along on his bumpy road and shares all his discoveries on his entrepreneurial journey. This book shares lessons that all can and should learn from."

—MARY MILLER, AUTHOR OF *CHANGING DIRECTION: TEN CHOICES THAT IMPACT YOUR DREAMS*

"This is a powerful read for anyone who dreams of being a successful entrepreneur. With his fresh, unique approach, Craig lays out the blueprint of how to build an international call center with a world-class business culture. It is inspirational how he invests in his employees to help them reach their full potential."

—CHARLES GILDEA, ENTREPRENEUR AND VICE PRESIDENT OF BUSINESS DEVELOPMENT AT C & G MARKETING INC.

"Craig's book shows you many sides of entrepreneurship, acknowledging the ups and downs with humor and perspective. One minute, you're surprised he's brave to admit some of the financial mistakes he's made. The next, you're inspired

by the investment he's made in his employees—even renting a real casket to help them visualize their future. Craig is truly one of a kind."

—MARCI SHIMOFF, NUMBER-ONE *NEW YORK TIMES* BEST-SELLING AUTHOR OF *CHICKEN SOUP FOR THE WOMAN'S SOUL* AND *HAPPY FOR NO REASON*

"I met Craig ten years ago on Necker Island, and since then we have traveled together in more than seven countries. Building a Dream Culture is something every company, big or small, should be doing for their employees, and Craig gives a great path to follow if you want to do that for your business. While you are building your company, you will inevitably have ups and downs, and he has great information on how to ride and prepare for the tough times."

—VISHEN LAKHIANI, FOUNDER AND CEO OF MINDVALLEY AND AUTHOR OF *NEW YORK TIMES* BEST SELLER *THE CODE OF THE EXTRAORDINARY MIND*

"I have known Craig for exactly twenty years as of August 2018. This book is an exact testament to his business journey to the top. I have had the privilege of having a front-row seat and direct experience with Craig's journey in life and business and can identify with the lessons and with the peaks and valleys he shares through the business wisdom he possesses. Anyone who calls themselves, or wants to call themselves, an entrepreneur simply cannot afford not to read his story and

learn from the high school boy and music major from Maine who has become an Extraordinary Man of the World."

—CHRISTOPHER RANDOLPH, FOUNDING MANAGING DIRECTOR OF THE SPORTZ PARTNERZ AGENCY; COFOUNDER OF GODSPEED TECHNOLOGIES LLC; FOUNDER OF THE TERRY GLENN FOUNDATION; AND COFOUNDER OF THE SPORTZ DREAMZ FOUNDATION

"This is one of the best books I have ever read on true team building. If you want a feel-good, 'unicorns and rainbows' view or any other fiction of entrepreneurship, this isn't the book for you. If you want a true practical and pragmatic approach to building a high-performing team of A players, then Craig's approach, structure, and insight will help transform your business."

—BENJAMIN CROFT, CEO AND FOUNDER OF WORLD BUSINESS AND EXECUTIVE COACH SUMMIT; FOUNDER OF ETHICALCOACH; AND COFOUNDER OF CONVERSATIONAL INTELLIGENCE FOR COACHES

HIRED TO QUIT, INSPIRED TO STAY

Hired to QUIT

INSPIRED TO STAY

How Focusing on Employee Dreams
Built an Exceptional Business Culture
and an Unbreakable Company

CRAIG HANDLEY

LIONCREST
PUBLISHING

HIRED TO QUIT, INSPIRED TO STAY
How Focusing on Employee Dreams Built an Exceptional Culture and an Unbreakable Company

ISBN 978-1-5445-1187-0 *Paperback*
978-1-5445-1188-7 *Ebook*

Without many people in my life this business would not exist, so this book would not exist. So many people suffer in the world of an entrepreneur...so I don't mean to exclude anyone because if you have been a part of the journey I appreciate you.

This book is dedicated to Glenn Reed who cosigned on the first credit card I could ever get for $3,000 and helped mentor and guide me in my early years. To my brother, Chris Handley, who started working for me fifteen years ago and took on and learned to fill about five key roles in the early years of the company; and finally my business partner, Tony Ricciardi, who has been loyal and trustworthy and a huge influence in my life.

CONTENTS

INTRODUCTION

How does a guy from Maine, who doesn't speak a word of Spanish, end up in Hermosillo, Mexico, an industrial town four hours south of Tucson, Arizona? In this case the answer is: opportunity.

If that sounds like an old Western film, it's not. You see, this is my story. The story of an entrepreneur who saw a chance to do something big and went for it. I, Craig Handley, am one of the two people who started ListenTrust, a call center company that began in the United States and made its way south across the border.

Though the company has found success, none of it came overnight. Like any entrepreneur, I've weathered many ups, downs, restarts, and turnarounds. I believe that the tough times are what define a business and make it great. The so-called failures are the greatest learning experiences in the world. We all have stories, and maybe mine will strike a chord with you and help you in your business. I am a music major who learned how to sell. In my own brain, I don't know if I deserve the blessings that have been bestowed upon me. I know I feel an added sense of responsibility...which, if I'm being honest, I'm not sure is a good thing. Sometimes I think life would be simpler if I were a schoolteacher. I could coach the football team...have dinner at home at night...but I'm not. I am an entrepreneur. (I'd probably get fired from the teaching job anyway.) And I think that if there were degrees handed out for life experiences, I'd be receiving a PhD, a master's, a doctorate, and maybe even a lifetime achievement award. I don't want to take away from what any of you who are reading this have done either. Many of you could graduate with me in the "life experience degree" category, right? So, these are simply the lessons I've learned in obtaining *my* degree, and I would love to connect on my website or Facebook page and hear your lessons and stories too. Being an entrepreneur isn't as much about me as it's about us.

Before I get into the details of the company and the lessons I've learned along the way, let's back it up a little bit, because no one becomes an entrepreneur overnight. At least I didn't.

I began my first foray into running a business as a paperboy.

While a paper route seems like a run-of-the-mill childhood job, it's an entrepreneurial endeavor. I had to collect my own cash and submit part of it back to the paper. Essentially, I was buying wholesale and selling retail.

One of the biggest lessons I learned during this time was the value of gaining new sales and how to sell. Every year, there was a contest to see who could gain the most new customers. I won twice. Once, I even went to Disney World as a reward for my hard work. I had no fear when it came to going from house to house, and that fearlessness has stayed with me to this day.

Throughout high school, I continued my route and did a lot of odd jobs on the side. I always knew how to find ways to make money. I have always been a hustler too. I got accepted to the Berklee College of Music, but the cost was outside my realm of possibility. But I don't take "no" for an answer, so I decided to join the Army Infantry to get college money. I got $750 a month so...that didn't really work out. But I was sure I'd get there...and I took music classes at other schools while figuring out how I was going to pay.

When I was in college, I discovered that if you umpired baseball games, you could make sixty dollars for each game. The games were an hour and a half, so you could make roughly forty bucks an hour. I saw the opportunity—I could either work someplace for ten bucks an hour and work forty-two hours a week, or I could ump seven baseball games a week and make the same revenue and still have free time. I chose to ump the games. I did the same math in being a ref for soccer. Games paid the same amount as baseball, but they were only one hour. This meant I was making even more with less time spent working. Choosing these types of endeavors gave me the freedom to enjoy college—do my homework, work out, play basketball, and party.

I have always been in love with music—I used to take over the hosting of local karaoke nights when I was in high school, started a DJing business in college, and ended up doing some clubs too. I realized that if I was DJing at the club, not only could I party, I could make money while doing it. I did this for some time, then started adding weddings, where I could make even more money in just a few hours. When I began DJing weddings, I only charged $500, but I wasn't booking high-caliber weddings. So I upped my rate to $2,500 and suddenly was booked all over the place. The best part was, most weddings were only three hours long and took place in the afternoon, meaning I had free time and more money in my pocket—and I could still DJ the clubs.

I guess you could say I always learned how to shortcut things, or how to work smarter. Today I call it the "side hustle." I did all these jobs because I loved having enough money and free time to do what I wanted.

In college, as I mentioned, I studied music. I wanted to be a rock star, but I was being taught things like sight singing and ear training—all things you needed to learn if you were going to teach music. So, I explored other options. I took some psychology classes and criminology, thinking maybe I'd be a cop. After three-plus years of college, I still wasn't sure how I was going to pursue my passion for music, and I still had a long way to go to graduate with any type of degree. One night over beers, a buddy talked about how much money he was making in sales, and he pointed out the fact that I had the gift of being able to talk to anyone. He suggested I try sales, so I started looking for a job.

I answered an ad for "sports-minded individuals" and I joined Combined Insurance as a salesman. W. Clement Stone, the founder of the company, had a system in place for new hires that was amazing. I learned more in that system than I could've learned in any other sales career.

When I first started out, I used to drive by houses searching for the right prospect. I was looking for someone who had a truck or a four-wheeler in the driveway, or owned a building company. I also knew that lobstering was one of the highest risk jobs out there, so I'd camp at the docks;

basically, I was looking for someone who needed accident insurance, which is what I was selling. However, that wasn't getting me ahead. I then realized that I shouldn't prejudge, and I started hitting every house and every door. I went on to become one of the best sales guys in the country. I won the company's Grand Diamond Award eight times in two years. Most people never achieve that award. I was at the top of my game in this company, but about two and a half years in, I realized I was trading time for money.

I was working about eighty hours a week, and the company only paid residual income for five years. I was busting my butt, and the biggest check I was going to take home was the one I was already receiving. I thought, "Man, I work too hard for $80,000 a year. I bet there are other opportunities where I can earn more."

From there I moved on to Aflac, another insurance company. I had about six months of living expenses in savings, and I worked with a friend of mine. We were trying to open some big deals, but there was a lot of paperwork and union rules, and soon I was out of my savings before I could replenish it. To supplement my income while I waited for the insurance deals to come through, I found a job at a call center.

The call center was a huge rush for me. In insurance, I

might talk to twenty-five people a day, but most of them would never turn into customers. At the call center, it was the exact opposite. Here, I had one hundred people calling a day, and they were all calling me because they wanted my service or product. All I had to do was talk to them about the benefits of what I was selling, and they would buy.

I loved that job, and it showed. Out of a thousand people at the call center, I became one of the top three sellers and held that position for a few years. I started writing my scripts, and others would ask to use them in training. Then I became a trainer. I trained people on those scripts, and they started to achieve better results. Some people eventually left the call center and became entrepreneurs. Then they asked me to consult part time. Suddenly, I went from making $1,200 a week to $2,400 a week because I had two companies that wanted me to work with them.

I became an expert at increasing revenue at the back end of a phone call, and I was in demand. I branched out into other call centers and other projects across the country. A few years in, I opened Revenue Enhancement, a consulting company, which eventually turned into more.

LISTEN UP

At some point, Revenue Enhancement was invited to be a

minority partner in a company called ListenUp. Our goal was to write scripts, enhance the value of their customers' experience, and provide alternative revenue streams at the back end of the phone call. My business partner and I had 15 percent ownership in ListenUp, and we had the bright idea to expand. While we enjoyed consulting, we realized we needed a center of our own if we wanted to stabilize the business. We didn't want to continue chasing consulting deals. Our first approach was to create a call center in the United States, but someone told me there was no one competing in the Spanish market. We thought that we could do a soft offer center, which was a call center that only took products that had no price in the ad, whether it was in a magazine, on the radio, or TV, and it really focused on sales skills. After we were successful in the soft offer Spanish market, people wanted us to handle hard offers and trial offers as well. Hard offers are the fixed-price ads you see or hear that say, "Call now. It's $19.95." Trial offers are ads that advertise, "Try it for thirty days for just $19.95," but the price is really $149.95. At the time, there was no good solution for any of these types of offers in the Spanish market, so we took all of those campaigns and calls.

I might not have spoken Spanish, but I clearly understood the operations of a call center well. At that point, my partner and I took the risk and created ListenUp Español. In three years' time, the company made *Inc.* magazine's 500 fastest-growing private companies in America. It was number one in the products and services category, and it was number twenty-seven overall, with 6,994 percent growth. In three years, we grew from zero people answering calls to 550, and eventually over 1,000 employees.

At this point, the other partners in ListenUp (the US company which was separate from ListenUp Español) wanted to focus on a software company they also owned and offered to give my business partner and me their 70 percent equity for nothing. We would be 85 percent partners with a product owner who owned the other 15 percent. The product owner was driving a lot of calls, and we thought we could make it work. Turns out, the product owner was leveraging his ownership percentage to pay a below-market rate on his calls and orders, which meant this piece of business was actually losing the company a lot of money. When the original partners relinquished their stake to us, it should've been a red flag, but we had the confidence to keep moving forward. My partner and I took over the entire company and put $700,000 into it, but in the end, we couldn't get it to work. Our call center in Mexico was funding ListenUp USA, so we shut down the United States version and grew ListenUp Español into what it is today—ListenTrust, an industry leader in the English- and Spanish-speaking call center markets.

BUILDING VALUE

We had a vision of what we wanted to create with Listen-Trust. At first, it was simply about survival. My partner and I both needed money to support our families. Starting the business together was the best option to do that. Our goal was to be able to make money and use what we learned along the way to make even more money. After a while, however, simply making money became tiresome. If your goal is always money, then you're constantly going to be facing ups and downs. Things became interesting again when we decided to take a risk in building a call center in Mexico.

For us, it became an opportunity to build something of value that took us away from consulting and brokering. We lit up, because now there was a challenge in front of us. We were going to build something that had never been built before, and we were going to own it.

Our goal switched from simply making enough money to survive to creating a brand and a business that we could fully own. As we grew, our labor force grew, and suddenly, we had to consider other elements of the business. The bigger the organization became, the more important it was to have systems in place so we could communicate effectively with the entire team.

Often, entrepreneurs have a hard time taking direction.

They like to do things their way because they feel like their way is the right way. I don't come from that mindset. I like to surround myself with smart, fun people who take advantage of opportunities and learn from experiences of the past.

This book is written from that point of view. I'm just a guy who's been blazing his own way; I got fired from every job I tried to keep, and most of the time I still feel like I don't know what I'm doing, yet I continue to be persistent. I think I've built a great reputation, and I've done the right things while having fun at the same time.

This book is my attempt to give back to more people. I believe the value of my life is in how many people I've helped to live the best version of their life possible. I'm not going to say that what I've learned makes me an expert in anything, but I've certainly put in the 10,000 hours that most people relate to becoming an expert. I think I have some good things to share. I asked an investment group that I work with to read a copy of this book before I ran through and did one last pass at edits, and they said that all the talk about "turnarounds" was kind of funny because their definition of a "turnaround" was fixing a business and bringing it way past previous highs in revenue. That's not what we did. They said I was more of a "restart" expert. In their opinion, that is a far harder skill to master, so I guess that's good? We've been able to build a kick-ass culture. We've kept our revenues in the $13 million-plus range every year for over ten years, despite the changing landscape of the business we are in, by reinventing ourselves every few years, and the tools we've used to reinvent ourselves are the same tools you use in a "turnaround." We've had over 1,000 people in our employment who we had to build a culture around, so will this book help you? I hope so. I expect you'll be much wiser for reading it, but I hope the story is cool too.

I believe you can do anything you want to do and meet whomever you want to meet. You can and should go after your dreams, but you have to work for them. You can't just say, "This is what I want to do," and expect it to happen. You have to be fearless and go after it. You must ask for help along the way, work hard, and reach for the stars.

That may sound clichéd, but about three years into the company, I began to learn about having a lifestyle business. I realized that there was more to life than just working, so I worked hard to support the life I wanted to live. For me, it was about adventure. I wanted to do the things I'd never dreamed possible. I went to Necker Island and met Richard Branson. I went to a culture event in Calgary where I met the Dalai Lama. I was the eighty-fifth civilian in the world to jump out of an airplane over 30,000 feet. I dove with great white sharks off the coast of Africa. I flew fighter planes over the Mojave Desert. I drove the

Baja 500 track through Mexico, and so much more. I've also met incredible people I admire—Paul McCartney, Jack Canfield, and the aforementioned Richard Branson and the Dalai Lama. I went to Ringo Starr's birthday party and met so many of the idols from rock bands in the eighties—it was a private event and everyone was just friends—the list goes on.

In addition, I went after the dream of being a rock star. I wrote a few albums and I still write today. I was offered a record contract, a bonus, and a tour schedule. I met Snoop Dogg and went to Akon's album release party, and started to network in the business I wanted to be in. However, life is also about tough choices. I had young kids and I needed to be there for them, so I couldn't go on tour. I did open at a huge venue, the Cow Palace in San Francisco, in front of nearly 13,000 people where Coolio was playing behind me. I hosted the Porn Awards. (I debated putting that in here. Am I losing credibility? Nah. Just keeping it real.) I played in Vegas and Miami, and I had over 3,000,000,000 plays of my music online—and one day I will win a Grammy.

I've done a lot of amazing things. And it's all because I learned that if I put it out there, any dream I have can come true.

I believe that if you have a goal, you can achieve it—an important message we impart to every one of our employees at ListenTrust, and it's the message I hope to impart to you. If you set a goal, you can achieve it. There's no reason you shouldn't do everything you've ever dreamed of. My hope is that by reading this book, you will learn from my mistakes and triumphs, and you will walk away with the sense that you can build the business and lifestyle you desire. You can manage the turnarounds or restarts that almost all businesses face at one point or another, and maybe most importantly, you can build a business that does more for you than make money.

A great business can enhance your life, but a great business doesn't happen overnight. I've learned that one of the keys to success is constant learning. This book is meant to be a tool for you to learn how to build to scale, create a solid financial plan, hire a dream team, embrace your partnership, move into foreign markets, and survive restarts and turnarounds. All these things are possible with a strong culture and a shared vision. This is what I know is true even though I don't always understand it. It is my story. I am still living through the rollercoaster of being a business owner and the Wild West that is entrepreneurship. Although I'm still learning, hopefully I can share my experiences to guide you on your journey.

Are you ready for an adventure?

CHAPTER ONE

WHY COMPANIES FAIL

One of the most epic and incredible trips I've ever been on was to Richard Branson's game reserve in Africa. At this point in time, ListenTrust was making $50,000 a week in profit. I felt confident that going away to see the big five game animals in the wild (along with the African penguins) was a well-deserved break. I had tickets to the World Cup semifinal and final and plans to shark dive, climb, and rappel Table Mountain. It was going to be an amazing time.

However, halfway through the trip, one of our clients changed course and cut their media. Overnight, our revenue was slashed in half. Suddenly, we were losing $70,000 a week and we were dumbfounded. To right the ship, we had to reevaluate all our costs. We had to work with our vendors to lower costs and look at the workforce to increase productivity while lowering costs. It seemed like a daunting task.

At the time, we didn't have a credit line or cash reserve because our company was still fairly new. We had cash in the bank, but we were burning it quickly. We had to call our vendors and stop payments to reserve as much cash as we could. We had 1,300 agents when we only needed 400 to 500 of them. However, we couldn't afford to let anyone go. In Mexico, if you fire someone, you have to pay them three months' severance. That means for every one hundred people we let go, we would've had to pay approximately $126,000. We had to do something different with the employees.

To address the overemployment problem, we cut the commission plan by 300 percent and decided to route calls based on overall agent performance. At the time, we had teams set up by product type: a fitness team, a kitchen team, a supplement team. Under our original scenario, the best few employees for each team were only taking fifty calls per day; by establishing a new routing plan, these top performing agents would be able to take up to two hundred per day. Agents were previously making around seven dollars a call, and under the new plan, they now made two dollars and fifty cents per sale. However, if you were one of our top agents, you were going to make more money because you would now have four times the amount of calls. The lower performing employees would receive zero calls, and therefore, no commission. While all employees received a salary, it was quite low. The commission is what made the job worthwhile. When we made these changes, many employees self-selected out of the company. In addition, by routing calls to our best agents, we improved performance on all campaigns. Media buyers noticed the bump and rewarded us with more calls. This accomplished two things: reduction in headcount without having to pay huge fees, and improved overall performance, which resulted in more call volume.

We then called up the vendors and explained the challenge we had run into. We iterated our urgent need to renegotiate and delay payments to a later date. These vendors would have to accept our new agreements and delayed payments, or they would not get paid. By accomplishing this, we were able to shave some key expenses from around $4 million down to $1 million.

While it took us a while to turn things around, we ended up having a record fourth quarter that year because of these changes. We learned that planning ahead and constantly watching costs of employees and vendor services is something we must always do.

THE IMPORTANCE OF FINANCES

So why do so many companies fail? One of the primary reasons companies fail is because they fail to understand their financials. They make more money, and they start to overhire like we did. We added consultants and advisors, and spent money on non-revenue-driving projects. When business is going well, you might not be planning your growth as focused as you should be, and you might become complacent.

Often, when you're starting a company, you're so focused on increasing revenue and business and scrambling to make it all work that you lose sight of what you're building and why. A lack of planning and discipline is why so many companies end up in over their heads.

In the call center business, the margins are small. Hence, the more call volume, the greater the potential liability. Key performance indicators (KPIs) are the most important numbers a business needs to know and monitor, as they indicate potential financial issues. If we take our eye off the ball as we're scaling and don't pay attention to our key indicators, we can easily lose control of the financials.

When we first started, we had one client who was generating the majority of our revenue, and we were incredibly focused on gaining even more revenue from that client. Because we had tunnel vision, all we could see was more revenue. But if we had taken a step back and looked at our financials more closely, we would've realized we should've been more focused on diversification.

We also overspent on the wrong things. We wanted to make sure we had a backup to each position, so we overstaffed. Most of our key roles got assistants. In one case, an executive's assistant got an assistant. We were making enough money that we got lazy, and when we should have been spending on growth initiatives, we wanted to look good...so we spent on PR without a real ability to capitalize on the PR. Ego kind of took over and we won all kinds of awards, but I'm not sure any of that drove new revenue or new business. We made all kinds of financial miscues.

As you're scaling, it's important to have someone with a strong skillset in finance. They don't have to be a CFO, but they need to be someone who can put meaning to your numbers. We didn't start doing this until later in the business, and we suffered because of it. When you scrutinize your numbers, you will see outliers that are warning signs of instability in your business model. If you ignore the numbers, it will be difficult to see that you're headed toward difficult times.

So, ask yourself this: Have you set your key KPIs? And are you watching them weekly? More on this later.

HIRE FOR CULTURE, THEN TALENT

Outside of financials, another reason companies fail is they hire the wrong talent, mainly people who don't fit into their culture. Often, when companies hire, they look for skill over culture. But some of the greatest skills in the world may not fit into your company's culture and core values. When that happens, you have someone with great skills who doesn't share the vision, and they end up operating out of sync with the rest of the organization.

Imagine you have a whirlpool with a bunch of Ping-Pong balls floating in it. When you turn on the jets, the balls start moving in the same direction and in sync. But, if you turn one of the jets around, the direction of every ball gets screwed up. When you hire the wrong person, it's like turning one of the jets to face the wrong way—it messes up everything.

In 2016, when the Patriots traded one of their best defensive linebackers to the Browns, it made the team better, because when this player guessed on the running back's direction, he didn't follow the instructions according to the company values. He had a lane, and they expected him to stick to his lane. When he thought he knew better and did his own thing, sometimes he would guess right and make amazing plays, but when he guessed wrong, he gave up thirty-yard run plays. He was the jet facing the wrong way. One wrong jet can lose the entire game. The defensive linebacker isn't a bad player; he's an incredible athlete. But in a system that requires a lot of moving parts working together to succeed, that style may not fit with the culture in that organization. We became focused on culture because we wanted to have the chemistry of a professional sports team. We had so many employees that we knew if one person was off, they would affect far more than a couple of people.

We used to think we knew what we were talking about when it came to hiring. The skillset and résumés seemed to fit what we needed, but we were basically hiring for good résumés, not looking at the values.

At the call center, we've focused on hiring for culture over experience because we're in an industry where there isn't a ton of talent that has the experience or desire to take on the agent jobs. So we've built our hiring process around culture. When we interview, we look for culture fit and someone with the same core values we have. Our mantra is, why waste time looking into someone's background if they'll never fit into your culture? The best way to find the right candidate is to hire based on culture and evaluate talent behind it.

For years, we weren't good at hiring people. Many startups face this same challenge. They're good at what they do, but they're not great at identifying the right talent to take them to the next level. When you start your company, you might just need a bookkeeper, then you need a controller, then a CFO, and you might not have enough experience to identify the right person. In fact, we've hired and fired three different CFOs.

One time we hired a guy from a bigger corporation. He had the aptitude, but he was used to working in a big corporation with a large budget, and we worked from a bootstrap budget. He wasn't great at working creatively with a small budget, and he simply didn't have the cultural fit needed to get the job done. In the beginning, we didn't require highly qualified people. However, the bigger we became, the more we needed a diversely educated and experienced team to help take us to the next level.

As an entrepreneur, if you're not good at interviewing, it might be a good idea to have someone else do the screening for you based on the job description. If we had found someone to help us with hiring, it might have mitigated the bad CFO hires. When you're starting to scale, talent that has experience building companies is quite necessary and prudent. To paraphrase Elon Musk, the founder of Tesla, when you're hiring, the only people worth hiring are ones who have made it through a crisis. In an interview with *Inc.*, he emphasized that he looks for someone who can explain exactly how they solved the problem at hand and "knows the little details."[1]

---

1 https://www.inc.com/anna-hensel/the-1-incredibly-detailed-job-interview-question-elon-musk-always-asks.html

Cameron Herold, the former COO of 1-800-GOT-JUNK?, openly talks about the fact that when he was replaced with a person from a corporate environment, they ran into the same problem we had. She was great as a manager, but she had never executed through a crisis. When 1-800-GOT-JUNK? came upon tough times, they had to fire her because she wasn't equipped to handle the situation. Herold admits he wasn't the right person for the job either, however. What the company needed was someone who had been through a crisis.

After going through several restarts and turnarounds at ListenTrust, we now see the necessity of having someone who's been through the difficult times. We've learned something every time we've been through a crisis, and we always come out better for it. That's why we hire for culture, because we need people who have had to work with a bootstrap mentality and who have managed through difficult times.

ONE PERSON CAN AFFECT THE ENTIRE COMPANY

In the early days of ListenTrust, there was a younger employee who worked a lot. I don't like to pick on anyone that has contributed to helping build the company, so this comment is strictly ability-based. This employee is an amazing human being who bled for the company. He was passionate about the business and a control freak. He controlled his business unit to a T and had a hard time being wrong. He fired a lot of people. At first, we thought nothing of it because he was such a dedicated worker. However, we eventually realized he was the problem. When there's a revolving door somewhere, the people being fired are usually not the source of the problem. Usually, it's the person doing the firing. Someone once said to me that he reached his level of ignorance. That's not a knock. It's a fact that at some point in a growing company, the people you have won't have the experience to go where you are going.

ListenTrust held on to him too long because we were afraid of the unknown. We were afraid that if we let him go, there would be a big gap in the business and it would affect us. Ironically, we let him go and everything was fine. Everyone should be replaceable within your company.

When you are faced with a challenge like that, it's best to let them go and face whatever comes next, head-on. If you realize someone doesn't fit the culture, then you should remove them quickly. Holding on to them is worse than trying to deal with the chaos they're creating in the team.

Terminating an employee always seems like a bad or difficult thing to do, but when you have clear goals and objectives, it makes it easier to know you're making the right decision to let someone go. Letting someone go is not about the person. It's simply about them not achieving their goals. When you let them go, it opens another door for them to move on to something greater because they're not a fit at the company anymore.

PAYING TOO MUCH ATTENTION TO THE DETAILS

While you must always be aware of what's happening in your company, there is such a thing as overdoing it.

Mark Stickney, a turnaround and restart expert, found that businesses are always trying to "pretty up" the details, and he summed up his perspective in his well-known saying, "painting the *Titanic*." In a restaurant, they're always trying to make the menu board look better, but if they're losing money, and they haven't worked on the P&L, there's no sense in improving the menu. Painting the *Titanic* is spending time on the wrong priorities, looking at numbers and the wrong data, hiring for experience and not the culture—in other words, paying attention to the scratch on the side of the ship when the whole ship is sinking.

ListenTrust once hired a financial guy who was detail oriented, but not in a good way. Instead of paying attention to our key performance indicators (KPIs), he looked at the superficial things. Our payroll percentage might have been at 70 percent of revenue when it should've been at 40 percent, but he was spending his time creating spreadsheets detailing the cost of paper cups. He was making things pretty and looking busy, when the bottom line was, if we didn't find cash, we'd be out of business in three weeks.

In every single restart and turnaround that ListenTrust has been through, we've had to narrow our focus to one or two key things to really plug the hole and stop the ship from sinking. If we'd worried about the color of the paint, we'd have sunk. Paying attention to the bigger picture is key to being successful, but paying attention to something means nothing if you don't act upon it.

COMMITTED ACTION

How often have you had someone tell you they'll have a document or project completed by Monday? Then Wednesday rolls around and they haven't done it. You ask what happened; they apologize and say they'll have it to you by Friday. Then Friday comes, and they still don't have it done. This lack of execution is a perfect example of someone not practicing what's called committed action.

Systems fail when people don't practice committed action.

My business partner took a year-long class through Stagen, a leadership development organization focused on business and personal growth. He returned with a document that we then used to train our employees to reach their goals and objectives by understanding and focusing on committed action.

At ListenTrust, committed action is the key to our success. We have about twelve moving parts to every campaign we do. If the setup team has to have something done by Tuesday, it has to be done by Tuesday so the training team can be coordinated to take calls on Thursday. If one group or one person fails to take the action they were supposed to, the whole thing can go awry, and deadlines will be missed.

If the setup team is late, we have a training team that's waiting for phone calls. If the contract is not done in time, the setup team can't start on time. If the contract comes back, and our sales guy didn't finish the contract, there's a delayed start time. If media has been bought and everything's delayed, the client's going to be upset.

When employees and management are trained on the principles of committed action, it makes a huge impact on the business, because everyone understands what they're committed to and how to communicate if they're going to be late. Training correctly on committed action makes everything move like a well-oiled machine.

Lines of communication are clearly drawn, and everyone

knows what they're responsible for, when to have it completed, and what "completed" looks like. If somebody asks you to do something and you say you'll do it and do it the right way, then it's done. When you turn it in, it's not half-done—it's done completely and correctly.

Committed action fosters trust. If one group commits to having something done by Tuesday, then the next group in line can trust that it will happen and doesn't need to watch over them. In any great company, there's a high level of trust among team members so that when they ask for something, they know the other person's going to support them and deliver.

Committed action is one of the simplest concepts out there, yet most people don't do it.

One of ListenTrust's core values is having each other's back. When the Navy SEALs go into a building, they might have three guys back-to-back. Why? Then they never have to worry about being covered; it's committed action in practice.

PERFECT COMMUNICATION

While communication is key, the right type of communication is imperative. Companies don't succeed by spending their time in meetings. They succeed by executing. Many of our meetings are no longer than ten minutes. During that time, we share the work done, the status of goals, and whether we need help on them or not. We call this our daily rhythms.

Cameron Herold wrote a book called *Meetings Suck*. In it, he explains that meetings suck when they're not run properly.

ListenTrust works well with conference calls and daily rhythms. We once faced a challenge where we wanted the departments that were in remote locations to feel like they were part of the team. But we also wanted to make sure everyone understood our KPIs and what we were doing daily to move the company forward.

Now we do a weekly huddle with our executive team, quarterly meetings for the company, and monthly finance meetings. Plus, each of the divisions has their own weekly huddle. These huddles help the alignment within the teams and eliminate emails going back and forth. We can bring up everything of concern in those huddles, and we can schedule a separate meeting if the problem is big enough to warrant another conversation. Each of these huddles is short, around ten to fifteen minutes, and we all stand during them to ensure they are quick and succinct.

Often, entrepreneurs will overextend their resources—

time, money, and people. They'll throw in too many ideas and opportunities, and they won't be able to fund them. They'll stretch their resources so far that they can never execute fully. The company will feel like they're working and assume they must be making money, but they're never actually getting anything done. To counteract this inefficiency, ListenTrust implemented a system that defines what we are trying to achieve.

We created categories for all tasks at hand in the business: Do First, Work In, Selectively Invest, and Delay or Ignore. We then place each task in the category. Then we assign people to cover each task. Each person can't be involved in too many projects at one time, or they will not get done.

This is a categorization that we've seen presented in different ways by many companies that talk about execution, so this isn't anything new. It's also been referred to as a quadrant box, but it's a good tool that is great for communicating objectives and goals that we are trying to reach on a quarterly or annual basis. The tool also ensures we do not overstretch our resources.

This system helps us prioritize what we're working on, what we should be working on, how to execute the ideas that should be executed, and shelve the ones we might need in the future. Everything has a spot on the quadrant, and if we add another idea or objective, something else needs to be taken away. The quadrant box is a great way to manage our resources.

MOST COMPANIES DON'T PLAN FOR SUCCESS

You can have all these systems in place—culture, a clear overview, and committed action—but if you're not planning for success, success may come with more ups and downs than necessary. Most companies plan for failure. They don't look at specifics of how they're going to scale or sell the company, and they lose their vision. They say they're going to be successful, but they don't define what that means exactly. They may say they're going to do $100 million, but there are no specifics.

To plan for success, you must work on your data. You must know where the revenue is coming from and have the right percentages for each department. If you have fixed costs, those might be 10 percent at $10 million, but at $20 million that's only 5 percent. You must go into the deep levels of detail of your finances to plan for success.

Early on, most businesses don't know the specifics of their numbers. They simply say they'll make a certain number in revenue, but they haven't fully thought out the logistics. You see this all the time on shows like *Shark Tank*. The owners will say they're going to do $20 million, but when asked how they'll do it, they don't have specific numbers.

They'll say they're going to buy Facebook media, but they don't have the ratios as to the level at which the media has to perform for it to be successful. For a company to be successful, they must know the metrics of what a successful Facebook campaign looks like based on the cost of acquiring a customer.

One of the reasons ListenTrust failed in the past is that we didn't plan the specifics of our success. One year we did $13 million in revenue, and we set the goal of doing $22 million the following year. Instead of adjusting our numbers to match this $22 million, we continued as we had before. We started spending money based on billing $22 million, but we hadn't yet made that money. If our percentage for marketing was at 7 percent, it was now at 7 percent for $22 million instead of $13 million—a huge difference. We were so over budget that we were losing our shirts, but we didn't see it. We thought we were within budget, so we hired extra people to hit our $22 million number.

When you plan to fail, you don't ask enough questions. You don't stop and think if you have all the information to launch the product. Don't let the passion for your idea take over and cloud the logistics side of the business. You must have both, but if you don't plan for success, your idea will fail to come to fruition. However, this is not to say that failure is a bad thing. In fact, failure is imperative.

We've had many opportunities where things haven't worked out the way we thought they would, and we've been able to look for solutions where most people think there aren't any. Entrepreneurs have grit. We have grit, and we know how to fail because we've done it over and over again. Every time we fail, we learn a new lesson and are able to turn our bad decisions into positive ones. The willingness to use failure as a learning opportunity leads to success.

Failure is only wrong when you don't learn from it. I embrace failure because it's how I've learned the lessons to help me grow. The more you fail, the smarter you become. When you don't take feedback, that's failure. When you continue to do the same thing and expect new results, that's failure. When you give up, that's failure.

When you can emotionally detach yourself from the company, you can look at it in a multi-dimensional fashion. As an entrepreneur, the ability to look at everything from sales to payroll to marketing and everything in between will allow you to plan for success. If you struggle to see all aspects, surround yourself with partners or employees who can help you see all the facets of your business.

DON'T TAKE YOUR EYE OFF THE BALL

When you don't have the right systems in place, and you

take your eye off the ball, shit will hit the fan. This is what happened when I went to Africa.

ListenTrust was making money, and I thought everything was great. When I came back, I realized we weren't as good as I thought we were, and the company wasn't as buttoned up as I'd assumed. When you first start to make money, especially money in numbers you've never received before, it can put blinders on you. You'll want to spend a bit of that money and have fun. While you've certainly earned it, you can't take your eye off the ball. You have to be humbler, and make sure the *Titanic* isn't going to hit the iceberg. You have to constantly stay on top of everything—the finances, the people, and your partnerships.

As the founder of the company, there's never going to be someone who cares as much as you do, so you have to constantly be involved. That's not to say you can't become an advisor, but you must always watch out for everything. You have to understand your KPIs, test your systems, and see the bigger picture. Even when you think you have the right systems in place, circumstances will change, and you will have to adjust.

All your processes need to be in constant review because your business is always evolving, and your culture has to be okay with change. Your culture needs to have the mindset that change is good and change is important.

You should be happy to re-inspect processes because they initiate change. When you become lazy or too comfortable, that's when you run into issues.

In business, you have to balance what you really want to accomplish with the resources you have available—people, money, and time. Executing through a turnaround or restart is just as hard as growing a business. It's a constant juggling game—moving pieces around to create a balance—but if you can keep your eye on the ball, you can succeed.

CHAPTER TWO

ESTABLISHING CORE COMPANY VALUES

Core values are like a compass. They can guide your business in the direction you want it to go.

By declaring your values early in the business, everyone in the company can move as one as you grow. If you have a set of core values that guides decisions—whether strategic or financial—chances are you'll have everyone on the same page.

When my business partner and I wanted to expand ListenTrust and grow as entrepreneurs, we looked at our company culture and determined that we needed to be more specific about our values. Seeking input and inspiration, we attended the Engage conference in Calgary.

I thought the conference was speaking to me. Culture! Engagement! I was aghast that they knew exactly what we needed. Of course, I later realized the whole conference was on culture and engagement (did I mention I'm a music major masquerading as a CEO?), but I digress.

The overriding theme every speaker spoke to was, "If I could do anything over again, I would establish core values sooner, because they make a huge impact."

When we left the conference, we were on a mission to create our own core values.

Core values are not who you want to be. Core values are who you are. When we started this process at ListenTrust, we set out wanting to discover who we were and what we wanted to carry forward that made us different.

THE DEFINING MOMENT

Our company culture has evolved over time, but there is one defining moment I remember distinctly. In 2006, the very beginning of ListenTrust, we lost our first big campaign due to lack of inventory. Losing this campaign meant that 90 percent of our agents would not take calls, meaning they would earn minimum wage without commissions until the campaign returned or we found a new client that was just as big.

At that time, we had twenty agents. I talked with them all and explained the situation. It was a difficult conversation, as I had to tell them I needed them to continue working in the company practically without pay for at least three weeks. I offered them more days of rest, up to a week, so they would stay, since I knew that the volume of calls would come back.

When I finished explaining the situation and offering what I could for a minimum wage, they left the office to assimilate the news and think about what the company had offered for their new salary, which clearly wasn't much.

I stayed in the office, worrying we were going to lose all the staff. I was trying to figure out what to do next, when one of the sales agents knocked on the door and entered. Behind him, all the other agents followed. One of them started talking about how grateful they had been for the company and about how ListenTrust treated them. They felt we were an honest and honorable company, and they let us know they were equally committed. They felt like family at ListenTrust. They made the counteroffer to stay to work their schedules as they usually did without importing the minimum wage. Together, they said, we would all make those calls come back.

In the end, the calls came back in two weeks, and each of those twenty agents eventually grew along with the company to better positions. That was a defining moment for everyone.

"I believe that at that precise moment the ListenTrust family and our culture were formed."

—ABRAHAM RODRIGUEZ, FIRST EMPLOYEE OF LISTENTRUST

THE PASSION TEST

At the conference, I met authors Janet and Chris Attwood. They have a book called *The Passion Test*. While their book was originally intended for people to use in their personal lives, they had been wanting to try it on a business. We agreed to work together, and they helped me apply their passion test to ListenTrust.

The purpose of this process was to figure out the answers to the following questions:

- What unique value does the company provide?
- How do we state it with elegant simplicity?
- How do we excite passion through expression?
- Can we make decisions based on these core values?
- Can these values be the basis of alignment (congruence)?

The process consisted of three phases. In phase one, we determined our core values. In phase two, we created a culture action plan and conducted passion test training. In phase three, we implemented our core values.

PHASE ONE: DETERMINE CORE VALUES

To start the process, we interviewed everyone within our company to determine what they believed ListenTrust's core values were at that point in time. They all had varying answers, but many of the answers were similar or overlapped. In the end, we came up with eighteen starting-point values. One was "Reach for the stars, never be satisfied. We can always do more." The second was "Seeing the need before it arises." A third was "True to others and true to ourselves, operating with integrity and honesty." These eighteen values were many of the things that had brought the business through some of the more challenging times.

When the list came together, my business partner and I sat down with our key decision-makers and went through the points, one by one. We said, "Would you rather be a company that reaches for the stars, where you're never satisfied with the current results, and you're always pushing to be better? Or, would you rather be a company that sees the need before it arises, where you see ahead of the curve?" We realized that if you're that company that sees the need before it arises, you're never going to reach for the stars. If you're reaching for the stars, then you'll be a company that will always be behind your clients. We debated each core value in a similar manner until we made our way through every single one of them and came up with the strongest answers.

Once we decided that seeing the need before it arises was more important than reaching for the stars, we went on to ask, "Would you rather see the need before it arises, or would you rather be true to others and yourself?" If you're a company that sees the need before it arises, you're not operating with integrity and honesty. If you're a company that operates with integrity and honesty, then you'll never be a company that stays ahead of the curve.

Would you rather be a company true to yourself and true to others, operating with integrity and honesty, or would you rather be a company that provides extraordinary value? If you're a company with integrity and honesty, you'll never be a company providing extraordinary value.

We literally debated each one of these eighteen core values until we had our number one passion for the company. Then we went through the entire list a second time, and we found our number two passion. As we went through it, some things blended into others, and others were eliminated. It took us about two weeks to get through the entire process.

From there, we determined our basic values, and we came up with our unique value, which was "Delivering awesomeness." This was our overall core value that everything then subsequently stemmed from.

PHASE TWO: CREATE A CULTURE ACTION PLAN

Once we determined our seven values, we set up markers to guide them. We made a list of action items that would not only show we had core values, but that we were living them. In other words, we created guidelines that established how someone would know if they were living the values.

We promoted the values one at a time and wrote a two-sentence description of the value. Then we wrote a manifesto, giving each value two paragraphs. From that moment on, every time we did something, whether it was attending a charity event or a sales meeting, we tried to use that activity as an example of one of our values. We use our values as our compass. Once we knew what they were, it was hard to stray from them. They keep us on track. If we stay true to them, then we can do no wrong.

Creating your core values is never a perfect process, but it's best to involve everyone at the company. You don't want leaders dictating what they are; instead, you want it to be a collaborative effort. Keep them simple and succinct so they're not left up for interpretation.

Fast forward eight years, and we refined our values even further. When we first created our values, one of our values was "Going beyond ourselves." We asked everyone what they thought this meant. When it was meant to be about charity and giving back, our COO thought we meant that sometimes we work harder than others to get things done. While his interpretation wasn't off the mark, it wasn't our intention. When we did a rebrand, we realized that some of our values could be interpreted to mean different things.

After that, we retooled every one of our values to have the definition within the sentence.

For every core value, we determined the unique value we provided, how to state it with simplicity, and how to excite passion through expression. For example, one of our values was "Living life like an extreme sport." For us that meant going all out and giving 110 percent; however, it could be interpreted otherwise. So, we rephrased it to say, "100 percent effort, 100 percent heart." The reason for this is that we wanted to have the definition of the value within the stated value.

PHASE THREE: IMPLEMENTATION

From there, we created a culture implementation plan. This plan designated one person in charge of each department. We created a mechanism to make sure all staff responded to an online feedback survey on the core passions, and we set quarterly manager meetings to review our progress toward aligning with our passions. We implemented a monthly call-in and created videos illustrating each passion. Each department then had a culture communications strategy, and we hired someone to be a Director of Awesomeness, who was responsible for our culture initiatives. This director created competitions, a hall of fame wall, dream boards, and a library to propagate the culture. One year we decided to do raffles, and every other month we raffled off prizes. For a full year, every other month, we gave away a car. We gave away six cars that year and had some great events around the giveaways.

> "I still remember when we started out with the Core Values. Craig and his partner wanted to create a department that would be in charge of promoting those values and also making sure that people would live the Passion Test. Luckily, I was the person chosen to run the initiative. Back then, I asked myself, 'Passion Test? What is that? Sounds interesting.' I had never heard about anything similar, nor had I heard of a company that would want to carry it out and make sure employees lived their passions, which was fascinating to me. Craig and his partner got totally involved in the initiative (he himself was the project manager), and we regularly had calls to check up on the progress, always truly excited to know how it was developing. That's what this company is all about for me, developing dreamers and believers."
>
> —SALLY CHAVEZ, FIRST CULTURE MANAGER

WE APPROACH BUSINESS DIFFERENTLY (THAN ANYONE ELSE IN MEXICO)

At ListenTrust, we believe people are the heart of your business. That is so cliché, right? But it's true. They are the lifeblood. Employees are not expendable; they are valuable. We treat our employees well because we believe in them. In Mexico, there is an industrial mindset where you simply tell people what to do and they do it. In an industrial mindset, businesses don't look for talent, they look for people who can conform.

During the industrial revolution, people's jobs were to manage machines and output. We are now in a people revolution where investments need to be made in people. When you focus on the people, the business and the work become more fun and fulfilling. At the end of the day, what we enjoy most about the work we do is doing right by others and doing well for ourselves.

Life was certainly simpler when all that existed was a small consulting company that didn't have to oversee others, but it was far less fulfilling. We now see that doing good for others is a great opportunity. We believe we have so many people because it is our job to impact these people's lives positively. If we do that, then everything else will fall into place.

THE POWER OF MANY

A business's power is derived from its team and the people it associates with.

Often, entrepreneurs put themselves into a closet. They become so focused on their initial vision that they forget the power of their network. Business is not the power of one, but the power of many.

I believe that branching out from my "closet" brings power back to the business. Too often, entrepreneurs get so caught up in the rat race of constant work that they forget it's okay to have fun. Getting away from the business and listening, engaging, laughing, and sharing experiences with other business owners in environments where you're not necessarily looking for new business is healthy.

When you get so focused on one channel or your initial vision, you shut out opportunities to grow. Seeking camaraderie away from the business is imperative. I joined the Maverick1000, a global network of entrepreneurs, because I was so involved in the day-to-day of the business that I needed an outlet away from the company. I wanted to be around more like-minded entrepreneurs, and I wanted to have fun while doing it.

The Mavericks fit my personality well, because it placed me around people who wanted to give back, grow, and be adventurous. When I attended retreats with the Mavericks, I had more fun in our business. I could think more clearly and was less reactive.

Whether you find your niche through a local or national association or through hobbies, you have to get away from your business. Being able to get out there and connect with other groups helps reinforce your culture and values as well. Finding a group or association that allows you to get out of your day-to-day routine is healthy, and I encourage you to find that. Whether it's the Maverick1000, Stagen, Genius Network, Gazelles, Young Entrepreneurs, or something else entirely, if you can find something that speaks to you outside of your business, you will be a better owner. Relating with people who are facing similar challenges, and people you can be vulnerable with who understand what you're going through, will make you stronger.

As an entrepreneur, you need to be able to think outside the box, and the best way to help you do that is to go into listener mode and learn from others. I've been fortunate enough to be able to associate with different groups and meet entrepreneurs from all over the world who've been tremendously helpful. As your business grows, you will find that fewer and fewer people can help you. You have to find different circles of people who are experts in growing a business. Everyone has something to add. As ListenTrust has grown, I've had to find people who are bigger than we are. I needed to find and learn from companies who have 1,000 employees and generate $150 million in sales, or $15 million plus in billings. (As a service company, we bill about 10 percent of the revenue we drive.)

My motto at ListenTrust is: operate from a place where you're constantly trying to learn. That's why I seek advice and mentoring from people whose businesses are ahead of ListenTrust's. I understand that I don't have all the answers, and I know we can only grow if we ask for help or seek guidance and feedback. At ListenTrust we are never complacent, and you shouldn't be either.

CHAPTER THREE

GOING BEYOND CORE VALUES AND CREATING A DREAM CULTURE

As ListenTrust grew as a company, we continued to nurture our core values, but soon found the need and desire to do something more. We were going through another restart and had begun to look at each division within the company to determine how we could increase revenues in each sector. When we came to the customer service division, we realized we were losing quite a bit of money. The key to making money in customer service is retention, but we were experiencing a turnover rate of 25 percent, which is quite high. That turnover rate cost us a significant amount of money, because while we could charge the client for training the first twenty people, if an agent left, we couldn't charge for training to replace that person. One of the primary reasons the customer service department was unprofitable was because we had trouble keeping agents in that division. We knew something had to be done, and because the problem existed with agent retention, we decided to focus on creating a culture that would increase retention.

We already had someone whose sole job was to focus on the culture—a culture manager—and we had our core values in place, so we explored what else could be done to convince employees to stay. We didn't have a lot of money, so we focused on ways that we could enhance what we already had in our culture and core values. We researched what we could do that wouldn't cost a lot but would make a big impact. We started small. We brought in someone to shine people's shoes for the day. We put silly pictures in the bathrooms. On hot days, we brought in popsicles. Nothing cost more than a couple hundred bucks, but they made an impact. People could see we were putting effort into our culture.

As we focused more on these small things, retention improved. At one point, I reached out to Tony Hsieh, the founder of Zappos, an online company known for its company culture, and asked for advice. "What else can we do? What are we missing? How can we continue to improve?" Hsieh put us in touch with his culture manager, and our entire HR team and culture manager got on the phone with her. The Zappos culture manager told us if we really wanted to make a difference, I should read Matthew Kelly's book *The Dream Manager*.

While I was reading the book, I ran into Jon Butcher, the author of a program called Lifebook[2], which talks about twelve pillars of success and happiness. Jon's mission is to teach people to be happy, and I wanted to integrate that idea into our culture. I really felt like there was a lot of crossover between happiness and dreams. Soon after, I met Reggie Chandra, an engineer and notable entrepreneur whose work has made roads across the US safer. Reggie had read Kelly's book as well and had begun to develop a system based around six pillars. Combining material from *The Dream Manager*, Lifebook, and conversations between us, Reggie and I put a plan together to teach people how to dream and be happy. I then took what I learned and applied it to ListenTrust by creating the DreamTrust. DreamTrust helps people not only to dream, but to handle their finances, work on relationships, and create goals to achieve happiness.

DREAMTRUST

Here is the premise of the DreamTrust: When we are

2 www.mylifebook.com

young, we all feel a life calling out to us...there are thousands of versions of your future self, and if you listen closely you can hear the one that is closest to your heart. Your employees had that same calling...and most likely it wasn't working for you helping you build your dream. I know none of our employees grew up hoping to answer phone calls and service others. It doesn't mean they can't live their dream life as a forever employee, but for that to happen you have to know what their dreams are. Happiness is a skill that has to be mastered. It's a mindset that one needs to practice.

I want people to believe in dreams—that life is amazing if you let it be amazing. It's hard as fuck, too. However, we have a choice to look at everything as good or bad. Honestly, some of the worst things in my life have created the best things because I focused on looking for the positives. I came from a middle-class family. I lived in my mother-in-law's basement with a wife and two kids, but I practiced and worked at being happy. I still do. And I want as many people as possible to learn how to be happy. That's DreamTrust.

DreamTrust is a program that focuses on employees and teaches them how to learn to be happy. It pushes them to go after their dreams. Whether those dreams are to start their own business, be out of debt, or something more personal, we help them set goals and work with them to accomplish those goals. A few of our core values apply to this facet of the company: Have a desire to improve. Be positive and fun. Keep an open mind. If you want to live your dreams, you should give 100 percent effort and 100 percent heart.

DreamTrust has a pretty comprehensive curriculum, but the main parts are the Six Pillars that help lead to happiness. Wealth, Health, Career, Time Off, Relationships, and Growth & Happiness. We focus on these six areas and talk about where people are in their lives. Then we talk about dreams, and we write some down together... and we start to feel the possibilities that life has to offer.

Part of the success of DreamTrust also comes from training our team managers how to manage not only with and without data, but also based on people's dreams so their management tactics are multidimensional. At the time, part of the challenge with our turnaround was that we were managing in a way that could be detrimental to the business. The way you discipline your team sends a certain message to other employees. When we weren't looking at our agents in a multidimensional way, we were losing some of our best people. Sometimes managers would dock people's pay by a fifth if they weren't on time, and those people were our best producers who were on time twenty-nine out of thirty days. It was no wonder agents kept quitting. Once we began to train our managers on the DreamTrust program, things turned around.

After the managers were trained, we hired two full-time dream managers to implement the DreamTrust program to its full extent. One had thirty years of experience in the banking industry, so she was an expert on finance, and the other was a teacher with a great coaching background.

The dream managers then ran classes and interviewed every employee that wanted to get more involved to find out their dreams and goals.

We had employees whose dream was to work Monday through Friday and get to spend the weekends with their kids because they were single parents, and they only had their kids on the weekend. In Mexico, that's a hard dream to accomplish. Most people work six days a week, and part time is so much less than full time that you can't get by. By simply scheduling them Monday through Friday, we could make their dreams come true. That was something simple we could easily do, but had we not had DreamTrust and asked people their goals, we never would've known that's what people wanted.

We also created support groups to help people accomplish even bigger goals. There were people who wanted to buy their own car, get out of debt, leave the business and create their own. There were others who were struggling with addiction or thoughts of suicide. We let people decide their own goals, and we supported them in whatever those were.

From there, we ran programs and presentations. During our first one, we rented a real casket and asked people to picture themselves inside. Then we asked them, "What have you done in your life? How many people are at your funeral? What are they saying about you?"

People became incredibly emotional, but more than that, they started to think about what they wanted out of life. We followed that presentation with the story of Colonel Sanders, who was sitting under a tree in his sixties contemplating suicide when he decided to sell his chicken recipe. We talked about Oprah Winfrey and J.K. Rowling, the author of Harry Potter, and their struggles. We presented real-life examples of people who had been through the lowest of the lows and still succeeded. We wanted our team to see they could make a difference in their lives no matter what age they were.

Word started to spread throughout the area about DreamTrust, and our turnover rate went down to 4 percent.

At ListenTrust we start all our trainings with the idea that our ultimate goal is that one day employees leave us to go live their own dream. We truly believe if people feel their dreams are supported, they'll give you the best work while they're with you. When people quit for the right reasons—because they found their passion or they made a career move—we celebrate. With DreamTrust, we inspire others to move forward. We also strive for word-of-mouth.

When people are talking about you, it's easier to grow a business. When you're doing good things for your customers and in the industry, people want to work with you. When you're doing good for your employees, and you're looking to hire new employees, it's not too hard to find talent because people want to be part of what you're doing.

HIRING WITH VALUES

Ultimately, the hiring process starts with the ads you use in recruitment; however, your values will guide those ads. If you can turn 20 percent of the people off from your business who are qualified but don't fit your culture, then you're winning.

When we hire now, we use our core values as a litmus test. We created a series of questions that test whether people fit our values. The questions are completely silly, but they work. For example, "A penguin walks in with a sombrero and a lemonade; what does he say?"

When we interview, we sit people down and first make

sure they can do the job. In a call center, we need people who are good at speaking. We need someone who can read with emphasis and enthusiasm. So, we have them read a paragraph from a script. If they read it as though they were reading a story book to a child, then that is someone who can read with enthusiasm. If they simply read it in a monotone voice with no inflection, we know they aren't going to work.

After that test, we ask our questions. Things like, "If you're stranded on an island and food and water are covered, but you're going to be there for a year, and there's no cell service and no power, what are the two things you want with you?" "If you're an animal, what animal best describes your character and why?" We are looking for unique answers. Ultimately, we chose questions that quickly weeded out the people who didn't align with our values.

We started shying away from using money as a recruiting tool and stopped revealing everything we paid. Instead, we simply said that we pay X as our base, plus commissions. We wanted people to be curious about the pay. Then we would bring people in and see if they fit our culture.

After the hiring process, we took a page out of the Zappos's book; at the end of every new employee training class, we pull everyone into a room and offer them a week's pay to quit. Zappos offers a month's pay, but since we were the first to do this in Mexico, and a week's pay is quite significant here, we tried it with a lower offer.

What we were trying to decipher with this tactic was whether someone was there for the long haul. After they went through training, if they didn't think we were a good fit for them, we gave them a way out. A few people have taken the pay, but we see that as a win, because we know the people who stay are the people who want to be there. They are people who relate to our values. Our values are important, and we use them as a compass to guide us where we want to go.

At the end of the day, you have to have continuity with your values in everything you do. ListenTrust does it with DreamTrust and in our hiring practices. Because of our commitment to the DreamTrust program, we have helped agents accomplish over a hundred dreams—ranging from starting their own businesses to losing weight to buying a car.

> "I think there is no other way to create loyalty, true loyalty, like the one you create when you tell someone that you trust him and that you will have him working on your team until the end of time."
>
> —ISAAC DYCK, HEAD OF CUSTOMER SERVICE, ONE OF THE FIRST FIFTY AGENTS AT LISTENTRUST

CHAPTER FOUR

LIVING YOUR DREAMS

Living your dreams is a process. In business and in life, it starts with the self. Before my business partner and I could ask anyone else to follow their dreams, we had to live our own. We wanted to show that if we could do it, then everyone else could do it.

We understand that living your dreams is not a perfectly crafted Hollywood story. There are ups and downs and long lulls, but we believe that living your dreams is simply never giving up on them. Your dreams may feel impossible, you may hit a brick wall time after time, you may want to quit or fold your company, but if you want to live your dreams, you can't give up.

Many entrepreneurs (myself included) turn inward when

they struggle. We want to figure everything out for ourselves. We may feel like the challenges we face are unique to us, but chances are there is someone out there who has gone through something similar who can help. Don't be afraid to look outward, be vulnerable, and speak to your close network about the challenges you're facing.

The amazing thing about humans is that we want to help others. If you don't have the power within, you can always find someone to lift you up. If you're feeling stuck, if you want to give up, you can ask for assistance. There are plenty of stories where someone is about to give up and another person walks in and reignites their dream again.

Be open to that. Be vulnerable. Be willing to admit you're struggling and surround yourself with people who care about you, who want to see you succeed.

When I was working for the insurance company, I read a book coauthored by W. Clement Stone and Napoleon Hill called *Think and Grow Rich*. The book presented the idea that the mind was not a fixed thing. The brain is plastic and can be remodeled. Today, this concept is called neuroplasticity. The premise is you can shape your life by believing the life you want is a life you can get.

If you write things down and say you're going to do them, your subconscious mind starts to figure out how to make them happen. You can literally build a life you're proud of if you focus on it and put it in your subconscious.

DreamTrust helps people do that. We get everyone in the company to write down their dreams and their goals no matter how big or small they may be. Elon Musk says we're all living as part of a video game being run by aliens.[3] Sometimes I wonder if that's not true, because whatever characters and scenarios I put in my head, they happen.

I was once living in my mother-in-law's basement watching my car get repossessed from my driveway. My goal was to have a successful company. I created that and more. If I can accomplish my goals, anyone can. Anybody can build a dream life they're proud of, whether it's running a successful business or something else entirely, it's possible.

Fear is the only thing holding most people back. To that, I pose the question, "What have you got to lose? Wouldn't you rather live a life full of the things you love doing than live a life that pays the bills but doesn't make you happy?"

With DreamTrust, we try to teach people that living your dreams doesn't have to mean you quit your job because you're making millions. Dreams don't have to happen on such a grand scale. Living your dreams means you're

---

3 https://www.quora.com/If-as-Elon-Musk-suggested-were-all-part-of-an-alien-video-game-can-you-identify-any-potential-glitches-theyve-made

brave enough to keep your dreams alive in your life on some level. Find the things you're passionate about and do them weekly. Don't let them fade away. Whatever it is that's important to you, don't stop doing it. You may never reach some extravagant goal, but you will be happy if you invest in living your dreams. If you're happy and you're passionate about what you do, there's a higher likelihood you'll make good money doing it.

There's beauty in living your passion. When someone is doing something they love, there's a different energy about them, and it's contagious. When others view that passion, they take that energy and apply it to their own lives. We at ListenTrust tell our stories, demonstrate our passion, and teach people how the subconscious works so they can follow their dreams.

A LIFE VISION

One of my favorite exercises in DreamTrust is the one-hundredth birthday party speech. We ask people to imagine it's their hundredth birthday and people are speaking about them. Then we ask, "What would they say?" We ask them to think about all the things they'll want to have done by that age. We have them write down what excites them and fires them up, the more extreme the better. If people only do half of what's on their list, they'll still have lived a pretty good life.

Most people take a job and think, “Okay, I just have to do this job,” but we invest in our people, and we want them to see that there’s more. We teach them there are twelve areas where dreams can be created.

These are:

- **Physical**—lifestyle habits, addictions, exercise
- **Emotional**—relationships, security, helping others
- **Intellectual**—reading, learning, continuous improvement tasks
- **Spiritual**—peace with yourself
- **Psychological**—overcome fears, insecurities, develop willpower
- **Material**—home ownership, purchase a vehicle, cottage, farm
- **Professional**—a promotion, develop a new product/service, sales/income goals
- **Financial**—become debt free, investment goals, financial freedom
- **Creative**—explore the arts, write a book, learn how to play piano
- **Adventure**—mountain climbing, exotic holiday, take scuba diving lessons
- **Legacy**—instill values in your children, volunteer, charitable giving, save the world
- **Character**—develop patience, walk the talk, earn respect, be worthy of trust

We present DreamTrust to our employees when they're first hired. We have them look at this list and write down three dreams per category, so they have thirty-six dreams to start. Then we have them go back and look at all their dreams and circle the ones that mean the most to them.

They then pick three to five of their top dreams and that's what they focus on while they're with us.

These dreams help create an action plan. Once people figure out their dreams, we work with them to achieve them. Not only do we inspire people to live their dreams, but we create accountability. We group people together who have similar dreams, and we follow up with them every thirty days. People who have health goals meet once a month and check in with each other to see how far they've come. The same goes for people who want to buy a car, a house, or eliminate debt. In these groups, people are free to be vulnerable and it creates a stronger culture.

Relationships build as people help each other accomplish their dreams. Everyone who's trying to lose weight supports each other. Everyone who wants to buy a car supports each other to hit their financial goals. There's a sense of brotherhood and a feeling that everyone is working together. Slowly, a dream culture emerges.

When we started the DreamTrust program, it was like

planting a tree. We put the seed in the ground and watered it daily. We gave it plenty of sun, and soon it began to grow. We watched miracles happen day after day. A dozen people have quit drugs because they had the support to enter rehab. We had a guy resign and open a boxing gym across the street from us to keep kids off the streets. We had an employee named Mario who left to join Cemex, a construction company that sold concrete. He became one of their top salesmen. Another guy left to run Uber in Hermosillo. There was a woman who loved to paint. She left our company and paints full-time now. She sends us notes that say, "I can't believe I'm living my dream. And all I had to do was do it." She was right. That was all she had to do. And that's what we believe. If you keep your dreams alive, you are doing them daily.

Living your dreams is being brave enough to keep them alive.

DON'T GIVE UP

Dreams are fueled when you have nothing to lose and everything to gain. If you have nothing to lose and everything to gain, then you can take risks, you can think outside the box and play with the big dogs. There's nothing better than a team that's supposed to lose that wins the game. Often, we found ourselves in this position at Listen-Trust. The underdog position is one that everyone can and should embrace. Because who doesn't want to root for them? When the underdog wins the championship, everyone cheers.

When we started, we had a simple vision: to be a call center for Spanish speakers that could handle difficult sales calls. At the time, there seemed to be about six to ten companies in the United States that did the same thing for English, but no one was competing in Spanish. We opened and began to take a lot of different types of calls, and the business started to grow.

We were never targeting millions of dollars; we just wanted a fun company with a few hundred employees. We surpassed that goal fairly quickly. We thought we would have about 500 people in the company and we'd answer 8,000 calls a week. We'd be successful, but we wouldn't be huge. We never thought we would do what we did. Our success was definitely not planned.

We operated on perseverance. We imagined that there was a wall in front of us, and all we had to do was figure out how to get over it, under it, or around it. When we could identify a route, we could do it. We hit a lot of obstacles, but we refused to stop because we always believed there was a way around. As long as we could see our dreams beyond the wall, then we wouldn't give up until we arrived on the other side.

However, what I soon realized was there would always be a wall, and I'd have to take the time to celebrate the wins, no matter how small.

CELEBRATE YOUR SUCCESSES

Living for your dreams will make you happy, but you must also celebrate your successes. As an entrepreneur, there will never be a horizon where you say, "Okay, that's enough." You will always keep striving for more. So, take the time to slow down and celebrate—not just for you, but everyone in your company. As a leader, you need to set the example that it's okay to celebrate your accomplishments.

As entrepreneurs, we're always looking forward, and sometimes we forget that other people on the team need recognition, time to celebrate, and time to recharge. To celebrate success or to recognize the efforts of others doesn't take much. You can send a simple email and copy everyone else on the team to thank someone for their hard work. You can buy someone dinner or point out their achievements in a meeting. These simple things don't take much time but make a world of difference. There's a quote by Philip McKernan that says, "There's no path to happiness, happiness is the path." That resonates with me deeply.

Often, business owners will have a good quarter and never

stop to acknowledge what they've achieved. They keep looking forward, asking, "How can we keep this momentum going? How do we roll this good quarter into the next?" Instead of always looking ahead, slow down, peel it back, and celebrate what you did right in that first quarter.

My business partner and I used to be on a constant cycle of "reach the goal, create a new one." Now we've shifted so our goal is one that can never be fully accomplished. Our dream with ListenTrust is to impact as many people as possible and to keep impacting more and more. The better we do, the bigger we become, the more responsibility we carry to share what life has given us with others. Similar to that superhero adage, "With great power comes great responsibility," the bigger you get, the more responsibility you have to do right.

That is a lot of pressure to carry, and sometimes you have to learn to let it go. If you do what you feel the world wants you to do or expects you to do, then you lose sight of your internal goals and values. You have to hold on to you.

There's a basketball pro who became a coach, and then a division head for Nike. He talks about how he was never really happy until he was sixty. Everybody thought he was happy when he was winning championships, but he wasn't. He became the happiest when he started to work for Nike because he didn't have to be a certain way. He didn't have to appear on TV, report to his team and the franchise holders, and hold up a specific image. At Nike, he was able to be himself and live his values without having to live the values of the expectations of the world. He was awakened to what was most important.

As entrepreneurs, we can choose to be something to everybody, or we can be ourselves. Shouldering that burden of responsibility can get exhausting. If you hold true to your own values first, then help others reach their dreams, you can find a balance.

A GREATER PURPOSE

Too often, we complicate things here in the United States. We compare ourselves to others, we compare our colleagues to others, and everything becomes a competition to gain more. If we could focus on the simple things, we'd be happier. If we could focus on our greater purpose, we might see there's more than money to be achieved.

ListenTrust has a greater purpose—to help others realize their dreams. When we focus on that, we're happy. We have our moments, because we're not perfect, but if you can focus on the greater purpose, then you don't get sidetracked by money and the like.

We've seen this in the charity work we do with kids in

inner-city Chicago. Here are kids and families who have faced much adversity—gang violence, poverty, and integration into the US culture. They keep trying to fulfill their dreams, but it's a battle. They may get knocked down, but they get back up. These are people who are still fulfilling their dreams in their own way. They have dinner together as a family. They laugh. They talk about their hopes. They celebrate the little things that are important, and they're grateful.

ListenTrust employees have supported villages in Haiti where the people literally have no money, but they have so much else. They have their families, faith, community, and their dreams.

At the time ListenTrust was searching for a charity to support, one of our core values was growing brain cells, and another was going beyond ourselves. When we found the BuildOn program, it was the perfect fit. BuildOn supports inner-city youth in troubled areas by providing opportunities for the youth to do service work for their community. The kids help people who are less fortunate than themselves—the elderly, homeless, orphans, and the handicapped. The premise of the program is that it gives youth purpose where they might not have had it. When they give their time to others, even though they're in a troubled area themselves, they have a sense of belonging and a purpose so they don't have to fall victim to some of the situations within their communities, such as gang violence. What BuildOn discovered is that when the kids help people who are less fortunate, it builds a higher level of confidence and self-worth.

Through BuildOn, we support a school in Chicago, but there are a number of them throughout the country. At the school we support in Chicago, the graduation rate of the kids in the program is 97 percent. When we began, it was 67 percent. Last year there was a kid whose parents were deported back to Mexico, and he was left behind. Multiple families took him in, and he reached his goal to go to MIT. By participating in the program and working hard, he received a full ride.

The first year we worked with the program, there was a boy who had dyslexia that was having difficulty integrating into his high school. Kids constantly made fun of him and he was contemplating suicide. As part of the BuildOn program, one of the activities he was tasked to do was to spend a night in the park with the homeless. He shared a night with a homeless man whose mother had committed suicide, and they talked about it. When he returned, he no longer contemplated suicide, because he felt like he had so much opportunity ahead of him—how could he waste it?

Just as we've seen amazing things happen with the Dream-

Trust program at the call center, we're seeing them with BuildOn as well.

We sponsor the program in Chicago because 2,000 students go to that high school and about 96 percent of them are first- and second-generation Mexican-Americans. In essence, we fund immigrants from Mexico who have a dream of acculturating for a better life for their children. Providing support to kids through the program not only supports their dreams but their parents' as well. For this, we are extremely proud.

One of the other great things about BuildOn is that they build schools internationally. ListenTrust built two schools in Haiti and sponsored a school build in Nicaragua. We even sponsored our employees to fly to some of these remote locations and build the schools.

For a week, we'd live in the village and build the foundation of the school side by side with the families of the community. They would host us in their huts and houses, and we were able to experience their culture. At the end of the week, they'd end up with a school, and we'd end up with a greater appreciation for the simple things in life.

While we were there, we'd have a videographer capture the experience so we could show the new school to the rest of the employees and celebrate together. Everyone had contributed to the funds that were used for the school, so even if they hadn't flown there to participate firsthand, they were part of the experience.

BE BIGGER THAN YOURSELF

To raise the funds to support BuildOn and the building of the new schools, my business partner and I realized we could raise the money ourselves or we could get everyone involved. We started asking the companies we worked with if they wanted to participate. We asked if they would use some of their corporate giving tax dollars to support our dream of helping others. We created incentives on certain products where we said, "If you buy this, then we'll donate a dollar toward the charity."

Donating to charity in this way not only got the companies we worked with involved, but the agents as well. Each agent was motivated; for every sale they made, they were helping to build a school. It gave a greater purpose to everyone. They were no longer simply making a sale, they were helping others. They were building schools and funding after-school programs in the inner city.

Doing good affects the culture in a positive way. We did a research study once where we created a forty-five-question survey to determine happiness in the center. We asked whether employees felt like their workplace was clean and safe, whether they had good managers, and if they were overall happy in their jobs. Numbers were pretty steady, but when we started giving money away to charity, suddenly the employees thought the bathrooms were cleaner, the security was better, and their manager was better.

When you give money away to charity, it makes people happier, which creates better results. With our programs at ListenTrust, we essentially proved that giving is profitable, which comes back to the idea that when you focus on the people, good things happen.

CHAPTER FIVE

BUILDING DREAM PARTNERSHIPS

Many entrepreneurs don't talk about business partnerships, but they should. If you're not doing this alone, then someone else is involved, and you should understand them. My business partner and I have a unique partnership, but it's not as unique as most people think. We were once asked to give a talk about partnerships, and it sparked a real conversation for many in the audience. Most people in attendance had never analyzed their business partnership in the same way they'd scrutinized the numbers of their business.

There are a lot of challenges that occur within business partnerships, and often the partnership doesn't last. They fail for a variety of reasons, including placing too many expectations on the relationship or entering a partnership too early.

A great partnership is one where you find someone who understands your weaknesses and steps in with their strengths. You don't have to have a partner who is exactly like you; you need someone who picks up where you leave off and vice versa.

My business partner and I are complete opposites, yet our partnership works because we have similar values and unique strengths that complement the other's weaknesses. We've been partners for fifteen years now. While we've had our ups and downs, the partnership has certainly improved with time.

DEALING WITH A CRISIS

During a life crisis, a business partner needs to assure the other that business is handled. One of our company values is, "Have the other person's back." In times of tribulation, it's nice to know we can count on each other not just for the business side of things, but also for the personal side of things. The business partnership is another long-term relationship. When you have empathy for the other, you strengthen that relationship.

When you're building a business, you will probably spend more time with your business partner than your spouse. Entrepreneurs are a different breed. We have a drive that's uncontainable. When we achieve goals, sometimes it's work to celebrate them, because we're always looking for what's next. Slowing down and realizing we've done something special is hard. Admitting we need time off or support is difficult.

Too often, entrepreneurs keep everything business oriented, but the personal is part of business. You don't show up to a nine-to-five and clock in and out. You can't keep your personal life separate. We all bring our personal baggage with us, and if you can't share that with your partner, then you will run into difficulties.

One of the lessons I learned with my business partner is that we have to be sensitive to each other's pain. We can't just sweep our problems under the rug. When you sweep things under the rug, resentment and negativity build, and the partnership starts to deteriorate. When you can speak honestly with each other, the partnership strengthens.

We have both been through divorces while running our business, and it certainly takes its toll. Instead of hiding this fact, we opened ourselves up, because we believe when you're vulnerable, you get through the tough times quicker. We've met with a lot of entrepreneurs who've been through divorce, and we know we're not unique.

Divorce is a life event that cannot be compartmentalized. If you're going through a divorce, it will affect your business and your business partnership. Business partners need to have empathy and compassion during this time. They need to give their partner space to rebound from the divorce and get their head back in the business. Divorce is a life crisis, and you may need to shift roles and responsibilities to get through it.

Everyone deals with the crises of life in a different manner, but to be good business partners, you support each other in whatever is needed to keep moving forward. Support can come in many forms—monetarily or by just being there.

A cool business partner recognizes when you need time off, space, or something else entirely. He or she sees that you're going through a difficult time and can talk to you openly. In a business partnership, each person should feel they have permission to talk openly to the other when they see these changes occurring. You should be able to say, "Hey, I think you should take some time off. In fact, you deserve time off to go through this." Most people will want to get back to the business right away, but a good partner will make you pause and think, "Am I really ready? Do I need more time to sort through everything that's happened?" Regular check-ins keep the business partnership healthy.

Entrepreneurs tend to rush back to the business before we've healed from the crisis at hand. Sometimes we need to slow down and care for ourselves. Other times, free time is not healthy, and a business partner should respect that as well. When you're used to running a business and going a hundred miles an hour, if you slow down, you may feel like everything is coming undone.

It's the partner's job to hold the other person accountable for taking time off and taking care of himself. Make sure that he's good and complete and that he's ready to come back.

Business owners often have it in their head that they need to wear a mask that shows they're invincible. But they should feel comfortable being vulnerable. Vulnerability in the workforce shows the strength of the leader. We are all human. A leader who can embrace that will shine.

You may think you can hide the toll a crisis is taking on you, but you can't. Your team will see right through it. Fessing up to the challenges you're facing is far better than trying to pretend that everything's normal.

UNDERSTANDING PERSONALITY

Doing the work to learn about yourself and your partner is important. If you don't work on growing together and focus on clear communication, honesty, and a common vision, your partnership will struggle, and so will the business.

Investing in your business partnership is an investment in your business. The healthier the partnership is, the healthier and more successful the business is. When you fail to see eye to eye with your partner, employees see it and the business struggles. When you're not in a healthy space, business suffers. When the relationship is good, then the business does really well.

In long-term relationships, there's 80 percent good and 20 percent bad. If you focus on the 80 percent of the other person's good, then you can typically take the 20 percent that is difficult and learn to work with it—whether it's values or personality traits.

Partnerships will not always be easy. You can respect each other, but there will be times when you become frustrated with one another. Often, frustration stems from a lack of understanding of each other's communication styles. When my business partner and I hit one of these roadblocks, we worked with a personality expert named Steve Sisler.

We wanted to understand how each of us communicated and how we could better communicate with each other. Sisler's test and program helped us immensely. So many people communicate in the wrong way with their business partner that eventually the partnership doesn't work anymore.

When we worked with Steve, one thing we learned was that we were completely opposite. If we were stranded on an island together, we could both figure out how to get off the island, but our approaches would be vastly different. By working with Steve, we learned how to better meet each other's needs. We learned to play to each other's strengths and cater to the weaknesses. Once we each understood where the other was coming from, we could communicate more effectively.

We also worked with Byron Katie, whose philosophy is that almost 100 percent of what you think is true is your own brain telling you stories to protect you from your fears.[4] All business partners will encounter times when they're convinced their partner doesn't value them, but the reality is, people demonstrate their appreciation in different ways. Often, they are being valued, but they just can't see it because of the story their brain has told them.

As a business partner, you have to recognize that you will never change your partner, so you must figure a way to work together that takes advantage of your unique strengths. We knew we weren't going to change each other, so we became determined to figure out "How can we coexist to build a successful and fun company?"

4 Materials from Katie can be found at thework.com.

ELIMINATING THE DRAMA

Drama creates dysfunction in relationships, but it also doesn't serve an organization. When my partner and I first started working together, we thought drama was funny.

The drama between us would always get people's attention. We used to constantly present an image of two people who were always at odds with each other. I don't think we were disagreeing as much as we were passionate about the business and put a lot of energy into that passion; however, people always viewed it as being dysfunctional. That dysfunction consequently started to bleed into the rest of the organization. We didn't realize it at first, but soon it became apparent in our culture.

When we were in meetings, we would point fingers at each other and argue in front of the team. Each of us wanted to be right instead of working together to accomplish what we wanted to achieve with the company. We would talk to other people about things that annoyed us about each other, but we wouldn't talk to each other, so there was no communication.

We were both incredibly passionate about the business. While we had the same goals, we had different ideas on how to reach them. We would argue over them and didn't have a way to express them healthily. That created drama.

Drama does not serve an organization, allow for growth, or perpetuate values. It eats away at an organization like a disease. Drama is contagious.

Your relationship, just like your business, will always ebb and flow. There are going to be ups and downs, and you have to continuously address and work on those. You can't just let them go. Make time for your business partner. You can easily fall into the trap of the busy aspects of your business, but if you don't set aside time to nurture your partnership, your business will suffer.

When there's pressure on the business partnership or on the business, it's more important to dive in and create space for the partnership. The healthier the partnership is, the healthier the business is. I believe partners should spend regular time together unplugged from the business. When my partner and I do this, our partnership is solid. When we get too busy and neglect our quality time together, our partnership suffers.

CONQUERING A CRISIS

When the business is in a crisis, you have to face it together. You can't point fingers or place blame; you need to come together and have each other's back. You have to have a mutual respect and trust in the other. This trust allows you not to have to micromanage the other; instead, it allows you to simply know the other will get the tasks done that they said they would.

When there is drama in the business, it's best to focus on moving forward rather than placing blame for the work that wasn't done. When you point fingers, things become ugly quickly and it demotivates people. You have to make sure drama doesn't enter into the business, especially during the tender state of a restart or turnaround when you need everybody's head in the game.

During a restart, you certainly need to pause and address what happened and why, so you can avoid the same pitfalls in the future. However, if you focus on all the micro events that are bringing the business down, you create a weakness not only within the partnership but also the business. When you're not united as one, you're not as efficient as an organization should be. In your business you will have many partnerships, and hopefully the biggest takeaway here is making sure you are thinking of your values before you think of the money.

CHAPTER SIX

BUILDING TO SCALE

Building a company to scale starts with a solid foundation. That foundation comes from core values and a purpose. You might have a great idea, but if you can't bring the business back to a greater purpose or a bigger vision, then you'll always be working in the now instead of working toward the horizon.

The worst thing to do is build your business and reach a level of success only to find that you've built the entire thing on a house of cards. When you build to scale, you plan to be large and winning from the get-go.

Building to scale is a mindset. You don't simply come up with an idea; you take that idea and have the courage to start the business. At ListenTrust when we start new business, we build it with the idea that it's going to be bigger than it is right now. When it is bigger, we think about how to continue to scale and maintain it. Our mindset is always, "We're gonna win!"

TURNAROUNDS AND RESTARTS WILL HAPPEN

When you plan to win, you hope that your business runs smoothly and grows without a hitch.

However, that doesn't always happen, and when you learn how to face challenges, you will become smarter and stronger. The tough times are learning experiences. It sucks going through them, but when you come out the other side, you have a new outlook and a new plan.

ListenTrust has been through many restarts, but in April of 2017, we had $500,000 in the bank, no debt, and looked to be headed to bigger and better things. Then the bottom fell out again, and we found ourselves in another restart.

We had built a new business unit based on one client with the hopes that once we stabilized that venture, we'd be able to grow from it. That business unit was a risky venture, and it didn't work out for us. The client ended up moving their calls just like they had moved them to us. We hadn't brought on other clients yet, because this one was using capacity as we grew it. We were even in discussions to give them equity based on continuing to work with us in growing our business. At the end of the day, they decided to move the calls to another center. We lost $470,000 in May, $250,000 in June, and $130,000 in July before making $323 in August, because we hadn't planned ahead.

To make it through this restart, we took the same steps we had in the past. We looked at what we could control, and we looked to bring staffing and key KPIs under control. We decided to keep some English sales agents on to be able to bring on new business, because we thought that would help in the turnaround. We brought in new business to backfill and focused on what we could control.

We certainly made mistakes that cost us, and we could have cut our losses a bit if we had cut deeper and faster. In hindsight, we should have done this, but we were always optimists.

However, looking back now, it's clear that every restart makes the company stronger. We've since increased our auditing and compliance of calls, and we've added more detailed reporting. We put in more processes and procedures to audit and manage calls, so we can operate with integrity and tell clients, "This was a good call," with confidence. We improved our sales processes. We also looked at how we charged for our services and created a new sales funnel that worked with the rate structure we were quoting.

These three things came back to knowing our numbers. Those numbers started to get better, because we now understood the type of business we were looking for, how to manage the sales floor, and how to structure our rates.

When you're in a restart, everyone needs to be on the same page, and you need to learn from your mistakes together. You have to have a plan to reach the goal, but you also need to be quick and nimble as things change so the little things don't throw you off track. To scale a company, you have to have the right strategic alliances, good communication channels, a solid understanding of your finances, and a vision of your future.

STRATEGIC ALLIANCES

One way you can scale a business is by creating partnerships amongst leaders in a category. When ListenTrust was first starting out, there was a company that was in competition with us in Spanish, but they weren't doing very well. Instead of continuing to compete with them, we suggested we use their platform and be their Spanish center. We worked on a strategic partnership with them, which later became a key to our growth.

Strategic alliances can also be looked at as great relationships, where you're not just buying or using the services of a vendor or a partner, but you're also potentially enhancing other businesses that use the company's services.

Working with our competitor was a great strategic alliance because we used their phone switch that routed calls to our center, and they referred their English-speaking clients who needed Spanish services to us. With that alliance, we received a discount on their service to drive calls to our center, and they could refer their clients to us when they needed Spanish-speaking agents. It was a win-win for both of our companies.

COMMUNICATION SYSTEMS

At ListenTrust, we need good communication, but we also need good listeners. In fact, it's part of our company's name—ListenTrust. We have to be really good listeners.

Our business is an ecosystem where everyone relies on each other to make a call work. There are a lot of steps that need to happen before an agent ever receives a call. From prospecting—getting someone interested in the service—to selling, to receiving a contract and setting up the account—hiring, training—to getting an agent on a call is a whole daisy chain of events. If something goes wrong in any one of those steps, the whole thing can fall apart. To mitigate problems, we created systems to allow accountability of that communication.

Every morning we have calls, or what we call huddles. They're short and sweet, maybe ten to fifteen minutes, but we communicate the major KPIs. If anyone needs to take action or get in touch with someone else, we bring that up in the call. If needed, we schedule a proper meeting to address bigger issues.

When we shored up our communications, we looked at a lot of different systems, and I encourage you to do the same. The system you use isn't as important as having a system that works for you. At this point in time, there are many systems to foster good communication. There are many online platforms which allow teams to communicate on a constant basis that are great. Find something that allows everyone in the company to know where the business is headed. Choose one platform that you can integrate across the company to hold people accountable and streamline communication.

Without effective communication, the potential for drama to enter the company increases. If there are ten boats in the water and they're supposed to follow each other, but none of them know the end destination, that's bad communication. If there's a thunderstorm and the boats get separated, they'll never end up at the destination, and you'll be running around frantically trying to track everyone down. However, if everyone knows they're supposed to be going to an island at XYZ coordinates, even if you get separated, everyone can eventually find their way. This is why everyone must be held accountable for what they said they would do, when they would have it done, and that it was done correctly.

COMMITTED ACTION

Committed action, coaching on committed action, asking the right questions around committed action, and having the right responses around missing committed action might be the most important things for scaling a business, because every person who is operating within a business is involved. For every action one person takes, a reaction takes place, creating a domino effect. If one person's late, then it affects the entire organization. In our organization, if we have a campaign that's supposed to be set up for the nineteenth, we hire agents and train agents for the nineteenth. When those agents are sitting waiting for phone calls, if for some reason setup doesn't honor their committed action of having the setup done by the nineteenth, we're going to have agents that we're paying for without phone calls, and most importantly, an unhappy customer.

If the clients have already bought media and there's no setup, and we have phone calls coming in without a script to take orders on, we're going to have to replenish the client's media dollars that they spent and wasted, because we missed the setup time. If training doesn't train well, then we can have another breakdown. If the technology and our computer systems are not set up right, and we have an outage, that could be the breakdown. Or, if the script hasn't been reviewed and looked at, that could be the breakdown. If the QA team doesn't understand what the compliances are, we may sell like crazy, but we're selling it incorrectly. When the client has an issue with the way we're selling, we lose the campaign.

Committed action is also honoring your commitments throughout the course of the week. On Monday, you say you're going to have something by Thursday. There's typically a check-in that could happen on Tuesday and Wednesday to ensure you're still in line with those timelines. That call could simply be, "Hey, Craig. Are we still on target for having it done by Thursday?" If you constantly communicate, you can constantly readjust the people around you who are counting on your committed action happening. Constant communication ensures that your team is communicating and focused on execution. When people commit to action, the communication within the business is good and runs smoothly.

Committed action is an important part of our culture because it allows us to effectively communicate what we need so the other person can effectively say, "Yes, I can do that," "No, I can't do that," or "Let me get back to you," and they can make a promise to get it done. I like to have a company of people and vendors that are more aware of what they say and what they do.

We're a more effective company when somebody in the organization can ask for something and another person can honor that commitment and say, "Yes, I'll have it done by this date." Now, that first person can go back to work and not have to think, "Is that person going to do their job or not? Are they going to get back to me? Do I really have to follow up with them?"

When we first went through this exercise, my business partner's assistant at the time said, "Geez, this is really basic stuff."

He replied, "You know, it's so basic, but that's what makes it powerful. Because nobody really does it. The more we make this a part of our culture, the more effective we're going to be and the more we can build trust within the organization."

Committed action is important regardless of the size of your company. That action is almost a ninja trick, where it's so simple that people don't think it will do much, but it's incredibly effective. When people commit to action, we also set up check-ins. In the check-in process, if someone fails to hit their promised deadline, you can say to them,

"How come you didn't finish this in time?" or "What can we do to help you meet that deadline?"

Sometimes when we work with our vendors, we might pin them down. We might say, "When are you going to get that to me?" If they say, "By Friday," we'll say, "What time on Friday?" It might be a little uncomfortable, but it is definitely an effective tool.

Committed action also turns everything into a learning opportunity.

Maybe the other party didn't communicate well enough and stipulate exactly what was needed and by when. So instead of chocolate milk, they were given hot chocolate at the end of the week because they said they wanted chocolate liquid.

You always get what you ask for, but you have to be really clear on what you're asking for. Stuff happens in the middle of the week. You might make a commitment, but part of the commitment is that life happens. If there is going to be a breakdown, your commitment is to verbally communicate that back to the person so they can make plans around it.

KEEP AN EYE ON FINANCES

To understand your finances is to know your actual costs

to operate. Understanding your finances is a major part of building to scale.

You don't have to be overly excited about numbers. However, if you're going to be an owner, then you have to be engaged in understanding the numbers. You have to know that the numbers are important and that understanding the right numbers is even more important. When you know those two things, then you can hire a competent person whom you trust to make sure the numbers are looked after.

It can take time for a business to understand their KPIs. For us, one of the biggest numbers to understand is payroll. We've been evolving and refining our payroll for ten years as the business has grown. Since we have a US operation and a Mexican operation, we have to look at the numbers closely to see the actual numbers we pay on payroll. While our numbers may have seemed fine if we looked at the agents we were paying on payroll, we also had many consultants and outsourced projects that should've been counted right away. We had to ask: if someone's a consultant, are they part of payroll, or aren't they? Figuring that out required us to ask the question: how quickly could we cut them in a financial crisis? If you can't cut them, then they should be on payroll.

We also learned if the project or consultant will be on the books for a longer period of time, they should be part of the fixed cost of payroll. We have an outsourced CFO group that was listed as a consultant whose costs we never included in payroll. If we had a CFO, he would have been counted. So we asked, could we fire this outsourced company? Technically, we could, but then we wouldn't have anybody doing our finances. We had to include that number as part of our payroll percentage to really understand what that metric was, and to determine whether we were within our KPI on that number.

As an owner, these are deliberate trade-offs that you have to make as you're looking through the numbers. You have to say, "Well, this is going to put me over my payroll by 2 percent. Am I willing to live with this trade-off? If so, for how long? Is this a four-month time frame I'm willing to live with so this sales guy can bring us business and start to offset that cost? Yes or no?" You really have to look at those percentages and understand what they're doing. It's the same thing with your marketing or your travel. If you see spikes in that, is there a reason for it, and are you okay with that reason? You have to break down everything.

You have to look at your reserve, and what that has to be to maintain business. As we grew over $10 million, we realized we needed a reserve of half a million dollars in cash. In fact, we needed almost a million. Our operating cost per week is $200,000. A million dollars is only a little over four weeks of operating capital if we were to lose everything.

Business experts say that for every $10 million, you should have a million in reserve ready to go. That is your oxygen in case something happens. Having a reserve is important in finances.

Another factor to look at is margins. What's your real margin? Often, you think you have your margin figured out, but then you start to look deeper, and you realize you forgot to add several costs. There are so many things that can cut into a margin that it's wise to consider them and possibly raise your margin. For example, you might decide to operate in a manner where you won't take a deal unless you have a 25 percent margin, because you know that 25 percent will drop to 15 percent really quickly based on unknown factors.

Knowing your KPIs and continuously checking in on them is imperative when building to scale. Your KPIs will constantly change as your business grows, but one indicator of whether those are the correct numbers is your profit and loss statement. That is a true marker of how the business is doing.

TOOLS FOR SCALING

There are tools for every part of your business that can help you build to scale. There are tools for building out core values and culture. There are tools to support your culture and tools for hiring based on your culture. When you focus on your values and operate around them, they have real worth. When you hire and fire by your values, they become part of the culture. Seventy percent of the worth of values is what you do with them after you put them in place. Some people may put a plaque on the wall stating their values, but if they don't execute around those values, they don't serve a purpose.

When you walk into a business that has a value system, it feels different. You can tell the company is grounded in values, and they know what they are. St. Jude Children's Research Hospital is a great example. You can feel their values from the moment you walk in the door. Everybody in the company knows their history and direction. The words they use set their attitude. Whenever I've talked to somebody at St. Jude, it's clear they know their mission. They're passionate about the mission, and it shows in their energy and presence. That's what sets them apart as a nonprofit. Having a value system separates a company that's providing a service from a company that is bigger than their service. A company that is well-grounded in a value system is usually more fun, better at getting things done, and great at what they do.

There are also physical tools for finance and strategy, and structure and growth, like the priority list (as referenced in chapter one) or committed action. Finally, there are psychological tools that will help you scale a business as well.

One of the strongest psychological tools we use at ListenTrust is moving outside of the business.

Being able to get outside the business is one of the most important tools an entrepreneur can use. The only way to use and optimize it is to step away from the business and let your brain think differently. Some people think I'm always jetting off and doing something fun and crazy that is unrelated to the business, but when I come back to the business after time away, I am a lot sharper. My mind is more open, and it helps me see the bigger picture. Getting away from the business allows me to get away from what's right in front of me.

Creating rhythms within the company gives structure to the daily, weekly, and annual strategies. One of the rhythms I think is important in business is fun. When you take the fun out of something like an annual meeting, people aren't that tuned into what's being said. Having an activity within the meeting that has nothing to do with the business is the same as going on safari. That activity is a time to let people's minds breathe and expand. Some of the most productive meetings I've had were meetings that included a fun activity that was outside the business.

When you don't have fun in the business, you're not having fun. Having fun is okay. Business doesn't always have to be so serious. It should be what makes you happy.

The book *Meetings Suck* written by Cameron Herold teaches anybody how to run an effective meeting. There's a lot of wasted time in business based on ineffective meetings, and it's a demotivator. If you're looking to make your meetings more effective, we highly recommend checking out the book. It will tell you how to run an effective meeting, which ones to run, and when to run them.

PLANNING AHEAD

The Gazelles refer to a "one-page plan," which is something we use at ListenTrust. A one-page plan can help keep the entire company abreast of where you're headed. A one-page plan has all your planning on one page.

You start with the core values of your company. Then you go to your company's purpose. Then you go to the vision. Those are the foundations of any company.

Once you have those established, you start going into your five-year initiatives and you define those a little bit. Then after that, you go back into your numbers. Then you go into your annual numbers and your quarterly numbers.

Then you have that one page, and that one page drives everything for the year.

You can then share that one page with everybody in the company. This is who we are. This is what we do. This is what we represent. These are our numbers. This is why. This is where we're going. This is what we believe. Everything is on one page and it makes sense. You can walk anybody through it.

When people can see the one-page plan, they are more engaged. They understand the bigger picture, and it gives them a reason why you're pressing for improvement in certain areas or making different decisions. The one page allows everyone to see the "why."

THREE-YEAR VISION

Having a three-year vision is a workable plan. Three years seems to be a good time frame because most people can visualize three years from now. If it were ten, it'd be difficult to see.

Visualizing a planet where nobody's driving cars anymore is hard, even though it's probably true that ten years from now cars will be self-driving. When you look three years out, you can get clarity and buy-in from everybody around you. If it becomes too SpaceX, then people might not take the vision seriously.

When ListenTrust worked on its three-year vision, we went through every department of the company and laid out what we saw in the future. We broke it down in as much detail as possible, asking questions like:

- What have people done?
- What awards have been won?
- What have you accomplished?
- What are some of the real accolades that your business has won?
- How big is your business?
- Is it efficient?
- What are the tough markets you're trying to target?
- What is your unique ability in the markets?
- What are your areas of growth?
- Are employees healthy?
- Are they going to the gym?
- Do you have daycare for your employees and their kids?
- Was that part of your vision?
- Did you put a slide from the first floor to the second floor?
- Is that something you want to do?
- Is that part of your vision?
- Do you have basketball courts on the roof?

Now ask yourself the same questions. What do you want your company to look like in three years? Your future could hold anything, and that's the fun of doing a three-year vision. Your vision then becomes the rudder on the ship, steering you in the right direction.

There's a YouTube video I love that shows a kid at a festival dancing like crazy on the side of the hill. Everyone is staring at him thinking, "What a moron!" But a few minutes later, another kid goes, "Screw it. I'm going to dance with him. He looks like he's having fun." That kid starts dancing, and then a couple more people join in. By the end, thousands of people are dancing without a care in the world.

When you start your business, you will have a vision, but not everyone will buy into it. Even your friends and family might think you're nuts. But, if you keep dancing, soon others will come along and join you, and by the end, you'll have an entire company dancing with you and your vision.

Building a business is creating a movement. Have a vision first, then you can create that movement where everyone wants to join. Once you create your vision, send it to everyone. Let them see that your vision is a great dance and you're having fun. Make them want to start dancing with you.

CHAPTER SEVEN

UNDERSTANDING CULTURAL MINDSETS

Operating in a foreign culture requires an understanding of different cultural mindsets. You can create the company culture you desire, but if it is out of sync with the local cultural mindset, you'll have difficulties implementing it.

Every country has its own quirks. When ListenTrust first started in Mexico, we had planning meetings. We would sit down and tell the team members what they had to do, and they'd say, "Great. We'll do it." What we learned was they would do exactly what we asked and no more. Mexico is such an industrialized country that they were used to being told what to do and then being required to do exactly what they were asked to do.

In our compliance department, we ran into the same problem. We told people to listen to a hundred calls. When the reports were turned in and we asked, "What did you find out?" The response was, "What do you mean?" We told them we wanted feedback on the calls and they said, "Oh, well you didn't ask us to give feedback. You only asked us to listen to one hundred calls, so we listened to the calls, but we didn't write any feedback down."

We then had to tell them to listen to calls and provide feedback, but then they didn't know what kind of feedback we wanted. We kept trying to give them directions, but every time we asked for more, we'd have to explain further. At one point, we almost gave up, because it felt like we had to explain everything so much that we might as well do it ourselves.

The mindset of simply doing as you're told and nothing more is one of the quirks we had to look at, but there are additional obstacles you might face if you're operating in a different country. Wherever you are, you have to look at the mindset and the culture. Are people more family oriented? Are they willing to work long hours? What are your employees' priorities?

You also need to take this into consideration with your vendors. We once met with a landlord who told us, "Don't worry, we won't hire any gays, people with visible tattoos, or men with earrings."

My business partner and I both looked at each other in shock. "You can't do that. That's discrimination," we said to the guy.

"We can do that in Mexico," he replied. We obviously told the guy we'd hire whomever we wanted, and it didn't matter if they were gay, had earrings, or had tattoos. But that was an instance that stood out in our minds as one of the toughest cultural quirks we encountered.

> "I had been working in the company for about eight months and Craig came to visit the staff at the center. I could see he had a strong personality, and I was kind of nervous to actually greet and meet the guy everyone had been talking about. So he approached me and said, 'Are you JC?'
>
> "'Yes' (with a shy intimidated voice).
>
> "'I've heard great things about you. You are a hard worker, and I also know you are going to school at nights, right?'
>
> "'Yes' (again shy).
>
> "'Well, you know, I respect that and if you ever feel like you need time to get your things done, I can always talk with your teachers, so they cut you some slack.'
>
> "That's Craig, always positive, funny, and inspiring."
>
> —JUAN CAIRE, HEAD OF SETUP, CENTER DIRECTOR

CRANKING THE WHEEL

There was another mindset in Mexico that we had to overcome as well. We called it "cranking the wheel."

One night, I was out to dinner with my team at a restaurant called Pancho Villa's. It was supposed to have the best breakfast in San Carlos, and we decided to go there for dinner as a preview.

We showed up at this place, and it was packed. We knew then that it was going to be good food. We were pretty hungry and asked, "How long is the wait?" The waiter looked over to us and said, "We're full," and threw his hands up in the air as though they weren't taking any more diners that night. We were bummed, but then another waiter came around the corner, and said, "Oh, hang on. I'll get a table for you." The guy walked over and grabbed a table with no chairs, swung it next to the window, cleaned it off, found a few chairs that weren't being used at other tables, and bam, we had a dinner table for three.

We sat down and looked over the menu. Ten minutes passed, and our waiter hadn't even taken our drink order. We decided that when he finally did come over, we'd order our drinks, appetizers, and dinner all at once. We finally flagged the waiter down. A minute later, he came over, apologized, and we said, "No worries. We'll order everything right now." We ordered a round of beers, some *queso fundido* with some chorizo and chilies, and our entrees. It was a simple order, except for the *queso fundido*—I didn't want any mushrooms. Everything else we ordered was just like it was on the menu. Ten minutes later, our beer came around. We decided to order another round because it would probably take a while.

A while was correct. Forty minutes in and we'd only had one round of beers, no *queso fundido*, no dinner, nothing. What's funny is there was a couple sitting next to us who came in fifteen minutes after we'd arrived, and they were eating *queso fundido*. I flagged the waiter and said, "What's up with the *queso fundido*? It's taking so long. The people right there came in fifteen minutes after we did, and they're already eating their food. We're hungry." He said, "Oh, really? Sorry." He then went on to say, "I didn't tell you, but the other waiter actually took the *queso fundido* they had for you before I could get it. Let me go put another order in for you."

I said, "Okay. While we wait, could you bring us something to nibble on, some chips and salsa and guacamole, perhaps?" The waiter said okay and brought chips and salsa, but not the guacamole. I said, "What about the guacamole?"

The waiter said, "Oh, I'll get you some."

I said, "Is it already made? Can you bring it fast?"

He said, "Yeah, it's already made."

Now, it'd been nearly an hour and we'd only gotten guacamole, chips, and salsa, with our one beer. We finally got a second round of beers and then the *queso fundido* arrived, but it was loaded with mushrooms. The waiter said, "I'm sorry," and he started picking them out. We told him that wouldn't be okay, so he took the appetizer away to get a new one. Then the dinner finally arrived, and we ate it. A few minutes later, the appetizer arrived. We started to eat the *queso fundido*, but again, there were mushrooms in it. I told the waiter, "It still has mushrooms, so we don't want it. And we don't want to wait for another one." We finally finished our entrees and the waiter brought the bill.

We brought his attention to the fact that the *queso fundido* was on there. We told him we didn't want to pay for the queso. He said, "Well, you ate half of it."

I explained, "Well, we ate it until we noticed there were mushrooms, and we asked for no mushrooms, and we didn't want it anymore. You just picked them out, so we didn't want to eat it anymore."

The waiter said, "But you ate some of it, so you should pay for it."

I replied, "We waited forty minutes to get a wrong order. We don't think we should pay for it. Take it off the bill."

He said, "Well, I need to talk to a manager." Twenty minutes later, the waiter and the manager were talking through the kitchen window pointing at us. The waiter finally returned and said, "Okay, I spoke to the manager. We'll remove the queso."

I said, "What about the guacamole? We only asked for it because it took so long to get the other stuff."

The waiter said, "But you ate the guacamole," and the saga continued.

This is what I call "cranking the wheel."

Sometimes cultures may appear backwards compared to your own, but that doesn't mean they're wrong. You need to figure out all the quirks and then find a way to work with what is already there. If the country you're operating in has a "cranking the wheel" mindset, your training program should be designed to unhook that mindset.

WORK WITH THE CULTURAL MINDSET

When you operate in different countries, you must learn how to build the company culture within each of those different communities. When looking at second locations to scale, recognize the culture, have a shared vision, and have the right people. No matter where you go, if you have these three things solid, you will have an easier time scaling.

One of the keys to our growth has been having agents in Mexico who have knowledge of the American culture so they can build rapport with customers on the phone. When we decided to open a call center in Mexico, we took the time to find the right location. Before we landed in Hermosillo, we looked extensively at Tijuana. Although Tijuana already had a lot of call centers, it was a better cultural fit because it was so close to the United States border that people there had a good knowledge of US culture. They watched our cable networks, understood our holidays, and bought US products. Plus, the majority of the residents there had family in the United States.

If you are working in any country outside the US that conducts business in the US, you should plan on building US culture. That means celebrating Thanksgiving and other holidays primarily in the US, teaching your team to find a favorite NFL, MLB, NHL, and NBA team to root for, learning about other US talking points like March Madness and the NCAA tournament, and knowing about TV shows in the US like *The Voice* and other reality shows.

They need to learn about US culture to be able to relate to the customers they are speaking with.

Also, no matter where you're going, you have to learn the cultural nuances. If you're trying to open a second office in LA and you're based in New York, there will still be differences. You can't simply open an LA office similar to your New York one and expect it to be the same. You need to look at the nuances in LA that you don't have to deal with in New York. Transportation might be one of them. If people have to travel during the day, they might not be able to open that office until 10:00 a.m. Similarly, they might need to open at 5:00 a.m. to have East Coast support.

In Mexico, people are extremely prideful, and they want to do a good job—almost to a fault, because they don't want to admit when they're wrong. Over time, we've worked on creating a culture where it's okay to be wrong. We let people know it's better to admit mistakes, learn from them, and move on, rather than to ignore them.

Once, we had a conversation with several managers over the course of a day. We sat with them one-on-one to discuss their teams and I asked each time, "What does this agent do well?" The manager would rattle off a list. Then when I asked where they could improve, they didn't want to talk about it. It was considered taboo. We had to teach the mindset that everyone needs to improve, and it needs to be studied and talked about. We made it clear they even need to look for those areas of improvement to build a great company.

When you operate in a different country, understand that it's difficult to change the cultural differences, because cultural differences are at the core of the people. Enter a different culture as a learner of the cultural mindset of the people that you're going to be hiring. Be patient and figure out how you will work with that.

GOING IN BLIND

When we decided to open ListenTrust in Mexico, we didn't do any research. We simply saw an opportunity to start a business service in the US Hispanic market. Because we understood the psychology of selling, we knew that the closer your dialect was to the prospective customer's, the higher your conversion rate.

At the time, 68 percent of the US Hispanic population had originated in Mexico. The logical step for us was to build a call center in Mexico. There were other call centers in Argentina where labor was cheaper, but we knew that Mexico would be more successful in conversion rates.

Neither I nor my business partner spoke Spanish, and the only time we'd spent in Mexico was on vacation at the beach. Together, we went down and looked at sites to start the call center. When we began, we leased a place that was low risk. We had to find a bilingual manager who could talk to us and the employees. We started extremely small and ramped it up from there. As we grew, we started to understand the cultural differences and that running a company in a foreign country would have its own set of challenges.

However, the one thing we learned quickly was that company culture gives a company a competitive edge in Mexico. When we focused on culture, we had a higher retention rate, happier employees, and better results. Combining that with our knowledge of the other quirks and governmental regulations, we started to do better.

THE "NEW" FACTOR

While call centers weren't new to Mexico, they were definitely new to Hermosillo, Mexico, where we had set up shop. Being a new business in a city is something to consider when moving internationally. Are you open to being the first company of that type in that city or location? Because your business type will be brand new to the area, you will need to train more people. Are you comfortable teaching people what to do? Do you have a training program in place? Or, are you looking for an established labor pool? And is that okay, knowing you will be competing for your employees with other similar businesses?

We wanted to be in a location where, if we taught people what to do, they would stay with us. It cost us a bit more money and time to get to that point, but it worked. Now there are a few more competing call centers in our city, but at the time, we were the only ones. There was a steep learning curve for us at the beginning, trying to teach what we knew. The skills we needed were an undeveloped skillset in the city we were in.

At one point, we had difficulty motivating our agents because we paid them too much and they were taking time off to go to the beach. In the Mexican culture, people like to take time off. To work with this, we incentivized people by paying a base salary and then creating commission plans. If they worked hard, they made more money. However, we made it flexible enough so they could choose to work less. If they wanted time off, they could have it, but they'd just make a little less money.

When we first established the business in Hermosillo, we went to the chamber of commerce. We wanted the community to know who we were straight from our mouths rather than through gossip. We went in and told the chamber who we were, what we represented, what we were doing, why we were there, and what we were striving to be. They were surprised we had thought about the community so much. A lot of the bigger companies that moved to Mexico had come to take advantage of the exchange rate and the lower labor cost. They were excited that we were interested in giving back to the community and creating a bigger impact, rather than just coming in and taking. Culturally, they appreciated the fact that we were coming in and enriching the lives of residents and not just looking at good economics.

GOVERNMENT REGULATIONS

Another thing to consider is the labor laws and unions of the country and how they work with your labor costs. Holidays are different. The way you pay people is different. The way you fire people in most countries (Mexico included) is slanted against a business. If you hire someone from Mexico, and they work for you for three months, when you fire them, you're going to pay them severance for three more months.

Then you have to watch out for people gaming the system. We had a group of employees who had other employees cover their shifts. They didn't come to work for five weeks straight, but we still had to pay them the minimum wage. Then, when we found out what they were doing, and we fired them, we still had to pay them for another five weeks.

THE EDUCATIONAL SYSTEM

In other countries, the educational system often doesn't teach the soft skills that we are used to in the United States. We were used to asking employees to think creatively about solving problems and give us feedback. The Mexican education system doesn't teach that skill, and we would never get feedback. Creative thinkers in Mexico are viewed as troublemakers or the undesirable. Instead of fighting that, we went after the troublemakers and the undesirables.

The education there also doesn't place a premium on being able to sell. What's interesting now, however, is that every company in Hermosillo that looks for salespeople recruits our agents as if they are gold. We once lost ten agents to car dealerships during a slow time because we'd taught them a transferrable skill. When this happens, we love it, because it's part of our values of going out, following your dreams, and doing better.

COMPLIANCE DIFFERENCES

Early on, the call center agents didn't understand what compliance was. They didn't know why they couldn't tell somebody that if they bought our hair product, they'd be running a comb through their thick head of hair in a week. In the US, there are regulations in place where you can't lie about a product in any way. In Mexico, the laws are a little more lenient. Agents didn't understand why we could be sued if they said one small thing that wasn't true, so we had to work hard to make sure we explained differences between the legal system in the US and down there.

HIRING EMPLOYEES

When ListenTrust first started hiring, we were looking for bodies, and because it was all Spanish-speaking, we didn't really know what we were looking for. As we became better, we tried to hire based on our core values, but they didn't know what that meant. We didn't find the employees we wanted until we started asking crazy questions and going to extremes to try to find people who would answer the questions in a goofy way.

Often, when you're hiring people, they come in and expect to be told what to do, and they do it. They don't expect to use their brains, and they're not expected to have any motivation besides making a minimum paycheck. We've had to work hard over the years to improve the quality of the people that apply and to hire the people that have the right mindset of growth. In the beginning, there were so many people that didn't fit in the culture that our business suffered. They were happy with the minimum wage. They thought that's all they deserved.

Early on, nobody wanted to come in to work. You couldn't

get them to work on the weekends. They just wouldn't show up. We had to put things in place to try to remedy that culture shift. We had extra bonuses that were given out on the weekends to encourage them to show up. One of the other things we discovered in hiring was that women are seen as second-class citizens. We put an ad up for a manager that said, "Any woman who wants to apply for a manager position, please apply." Only one woman applied.

SLOW DOWN

In Mexico, everything moves at a slower pace. As a gringo and an entrepreneur, and in the industry I'm in, I need results now. Being patient with the process was a learning experience.

In Mexico, schmoozing is really important. They don't want to rush into business over dinner. It takes time to get to that part of the conversation. If you rush, it's an insult. They want to get to know you before they talk business.

Slowing down and figuring out the Mexican culture was also a serious investment. ListenTrust burned through a lot of cash trying to understand everything. When you're building a call center, you can't abandon calls. However, there weren't a lot of routing tools that we could use to route calls to another call center. Business was up and down until we aligned with a strategic partner that helped us grow.

LANGUAGE DOESN'T HAVE TO BE A BARRIER

You don't have to speak the language to open a business in a different country. ListenTrust is twelve years into its operation in Mexico, and I still don't speak the language. Using translators is not a big deal.

However, when we first started, every interview my business partner and I did for the media brought up the fact that we didn't speak Spanish. They'd want to know how we built and managed a call center in a country where we didn't even speak the language.

I'm still amazed that we can sit through day-long meetings with a translator who's able to go back and forth between English and Spanish for both sides. Things might have been better if we'd learned Spanish, but that was never a priority. Our priority was the people. By paying attention to the Mexican culture and working with its quirks to create our own dream culture, we were able to succeed.

CHAPTER EIGHT

SURVIVING RESTARTS

This chapter was originally called "Surviving Turnarounds," but if you define a "turnaround" as fixing cash, ListenTrust is a company in an ever-changing business environment. We started in Spanish and sales calls from Spanish-speaking customers, and as that ebbed and flowed and those buyers started to go online, we needed to add calls. As revenue fell, we needed to find ways to remold our business to maintain the revenues, so we would have a great year and an off year, a great year and an off year. Despite the ups and downs, we maintained $13 million-plus in revenue year over year. Some years to get the revenue, our expenses increased, which is why profits would go up and down. Whether you call it a turnaround or a restart, I think we have a pretty good grip on how to stay alive in business.

No matter how good you might think you are, everyone will face rough spots in their business and will go through a financial crisis or even many financial crises at some point. The secret to surviving is being willing and able to look at a variety of different solutions. Usually, there is not one solution to the problem at hand but many. Any solution that allows the company to keep paying the bills should be considered.

When you enter a restart, you need to let everyone know what is happening. Once you develop a plan to prevent the company from going bankrupt, then you need to communicate that plan. When ListenTrust is in a turnaround, we make sure to let everyone know that we're in a difficult spot. We also let them know the reasoning behind our decisions.

In our last restart we had to let some senior executives go so we could keep our agents. We let the agents know we let these people go so we could keep them on. We explained that we knew the agents were the ones generating the revenue, and we made this clear to them. By being transparent, we inspired them to want to excel. They understood the importance of every call they took. We pulled everyone together so they realized the challenges we were facing and what their role was going to be in helping us overcome those challenges. We also encouraged every department to bring any cost-saving ideas to us.

During financial challenges, you have to live with faith. You have to believe that if you make your best effort and focus on what you can control, you can overcome the problem. ListenTrust was once in a position where we were losing $15,000 per day. Some people would panic over that, but we did not. We realized it was part of the process, and we made decisions that we could control to try to control the losses. We made decisions that increased revenue and lowered expenses until we could return the company to a profitable state.

I believe you have to keep trying and doing your best. If it's not meant to be, then you won't overcome it. Do what you can do to the best of your ability and hope that things fall into place. Heck, if it doesn't work, there's nothing more you can do, because you controlled what you could control.

PREPARING FOR A RESTART

One of the best ways to be prepared for a restart is to focus on your finances.

Having a cash reserve in the bank and a credit line will ensure you have enough money to make it through the turnaround. Surviving a turnaround is like scuba diving, and that cash is the oxygen in the tank. If you dive to one hundred feet and you're not paying attention, you might not have enough oxygen to get back to the surface.

If you're a $10 million company, you need a half-million-dollar credit line and maybe $300,000 in the bank. If you're a $15 million company, you need a half-million-dollar credit line, and a half million dollars in the bank. Basically, you want $1 million dollars in cash for every $10 million that you're doing in revenue to protect yourself from going out of business if negative events happen.

There was one point in our business where we made $600,000 in the first quarter. My partner and I could have each taken $300,000 and done a lot with that money, but we kept it in the company, because we recognized we could have a bad summer and we might need it. If we didn't have that money in the bank, there wouldn't be a business today. We had a credit line of a half million dollars, and we would've had to take out a loan at a high interest rate. We might have survived, but it would've been difficult. However, because we thought ahead and paid attention to our finances, we had $600,000 in reserve in the bank.

When ListenTrust started losing money five months later, we didn't have to panic, because we knew we were cutting through our profits from the first quarter, which was monopoly money to us. That doesn't mean the money wasn't real, but it was less real because we never saw it. If we'd taken that money out of the company, it would've hit us much harder when we had to put the money back into the company.

Cash flow is king. You have a list of payables. If necessary, stop paying your payables. Keep the cash in the business to operate. This might sound like a bad thing but your vendors rely on you to keep their revenues going. They will all work with you to help you keep your business alive. We pay a huge fee for long distance, platform fees, legal, and many more. The list isn't huge, but it's pretty big. When necessary (and it usually is), we stop paying all those bills. We agree to keep them current going forward and pay them off a little each month when we have the cash. Vendors have two options. Say no and put you out of business so you can't ever pay them, or work with you to support you in your restart. They may want to know why you are in the situation you are in and your plan to fix it, but that's why they are your partners: to help you get through this grueling cash need. I am not saying don't pay your vendors. We've never not paid our bills, even on a handshake deal. I am saying that you have more options than you are probably aware of to stay alive and fix things.

EXECUTING IN A RESTART

Some entrepreneurs are optimistic in a restart, which is great, but it's always good to check your optimism against your forecasts. When ListenTrust is in a restart, we look at our numbers differently. Instead of looking month to month, we look at week to week. We forecast our budget out against our sales forecast, and then we drill down into the sales forecast. We look at the big picture, and then we bring it down to a micro level, so everybody understands what they need to do and why they need to do it. Our measuring systems in a turnaround are more micro because we're managing money week to week, if not day to day. We have to be conservative with our sales forecast, new cash flow, and the timeline of the cash flow. We can't be overly optimistic, because that will bite us in the butt, we'll run out of money, and we'll be done.

In a restart, the temperature in the organization should be positive but also real. Make sure everybody understands you are in a very tender situation in the company. Things will be heightened and looked at differently. Everything has to be executed on. There is no room for error. Since there is not a lot of room for error, you can only take on the most profitable prospects during this time. Focus on a few key priorities and the plan of the restart, keeping it simple.

ListenTrust once worked with a flower company that we enjoyed doing business with. They started with us in September, and for four months, everything went smoothly. They paid their invoices like clockwork, and we delivered what we promised.

After those four months, they told us they loved doing business with us, and they wanted to shut down their facilities in the Philippines and Honduras and do 100 percent of their work with us. They asked if it was possible for us to get 400 agents for Valentine's Day. We put a plan together that basically covered our break-even costs, and everything after that was incentive driven. If we could get agents who were able to meet the staffing requirements and hit sales goals, there was different revenue that we could create. All in, it should have brought us a workable hourly rate.

We decided this was a great opportunity and opened a new center in a different country for this client. The majority of the business for that build-out and that investment was based on this client, which was the reason why we were going to Belize. We made a large investment with the hopes that we would make money over a period of time. We thought we would be able to leverage that investment to get more business in Belize and that our leap of faith would pay off. We understood that in the beginning months it wouldn't make us any money. However, we viewed it as an opportunity to help us expand and pivot into a different country that had more English capabilities.

The flower company agreed to the plan, and we truly felt like this would be a good joint partnership. However, from the moment we started working with them on the new plan, everything that happened felt like they were trying to work against us, even down to hiring. We'd hire people, and they'd fire them the next day.

At the end of January that year, we sent them an invoice. They told us they didn't agree 100 percent with the invoice we sent. They said they'd only agree to a smaller number. That smaller number wasn't enough. Our payroll alone was $290,000, and they had sent us $230,000 for January. Their payment didn't cover any costs; in fact, it didn't even cover our payroll.

We confronted them, and they said, "Well, we can send you this small amount or we can discuss it after Valentine's Day, because Valentine's Day is next week." Of course, we needed the cash, so we said, "Well, send that amount, and we'll discuss it after Valentine's Day."

Valentine's came and went. By the end of February, they said, "The money's coming." We finally said, "Look, we're in the second week of March, and you haven't paid. We need our money."

They came back and said, "Well, we don't agree with how you're billing us, so just talk to our lawyers." We had literally put out close to $650,000 in agent pay alone, and they had only given us $230,000.

When we added in the potential bonuses, the estimates

were that it was around $850,000 to $1,000,000 that we were owed. We couldn't argue, however, because they didn't give us any reporting. They shut us off on all the reporting right at Valentine's Day, so we couldn't even look to see what we thought we should be receiving. One of our bonuses was on compliance and apparently 100 percent of our agents had bad calls. We had a conversation with their customer service manager who actually admitted that "We don't actually listen to calls."

She told us that "We just have a quota where we have to find three things wrong with every agent or we get fired." We were never going to receive a bonus on quality. It was mathematically impossible for them to listen to all the calls they received during that week.

There were bonuses we should have received, but because they said, "Oh, no, everybody did something wrong," we received nothing. We ended up having to sue them. At the time, we needed the cash, so we already knew we were going to take whatever they offered. The eventual settlement was not enough.

We were about three days away from not making payroll at the call center. We had already stopped our US payroll for the previous three weeks. We took out a loan at the last minute at 14 percent and with a huge fee up front. That money was able to give us oxygen.

Once we had the money, we had the space and time to go to the center and look at what we were going to do to fix the problem. When we explored each division, we found our shortcomings. In customer service, for example, our clients were managing a lot of our billings, and they were logging agents on and off. Our agents would be sitting in the seats, and we would have to pay for those agents. But the client would say, "Well, I don't have to pay for them unless they're logged on." We said, "Well, we're losing money." We weren't paying close enough attention to our finances, and we were losing about $17,000 by taking other companies' customer service calls. Even though we were billing out a large sum and making revenue, we weren't looking at our margins. We didn't know that for every single dollar we were billing in revenue, we were losing close to seventy cents. Once we looked closer at our numbers, we were able to put a plan in place to improve performance.

Along with customer service, we talked to all our clients about how they were billing us and how we were billing them. We explained exactly what was going on with our company so that we'd stop losing money. We turned billing from a loss into around $24,000 a week in revenue, which added revenue to the bottom line. After about four to six weeks, we were able to turn everything from a loss position into a revenue-generating position. The money coming in wasn't a lot, but it was better than losing money every week.

Another thing we looked at were our expenses. In a restart, it's equally if not more important to cut expenses everywhere you can, because that adds hard dollars to your bottom line. Often, entrepreneurs find themselves in a restart and are inclined to make more to solve their problem, but you make your money in a turnaround by cutting expenses, not billing more. For every dollar you save, you make a dollar. For every dollar you get in revenue, you only receive your margin—for us that might only mean eighteen to twenty cents. If we cut $20,000 in expenses, we now have $20,000 in cash. If, however, we bill $20,000 we might only make $4,000.

Another factor we considered in the restart was our performance in Spanish. We added some incentives for additional performance that created an extra bump in revenue every week. Then we decided to go against our strategy and add English sales. We asked one of our clients if they would give us some call volume. We performed really well, and they gave us more call volume. We ended up paying off the loan and our credit line within about three and a half months. In the end, we ended up having a year where we did over $1 million in profit.

In that particular restart, or giant financial hole, we looked at each division and its finances. We tried to make sure each one of our different revenue-generating divisions was generating a profitable revenue. When they weren't, we tried to fix each division independently. One of my favorite quotes is "using little hinges to swing big doors." Each one of those things, we looked at as a hinge. We were trying to generate $30,000 in revenue in each division. That would create $90,000 a week in positive revenue, which would be added to the bottom line and create a plan that would help us generate a profitable year. Along with all of that, we also made as many cuts as we could. We went through every expense and tried to minimize those expenses.

Before we ended up taking out that unsecured loan, we had a plan. We had a plan of cash flow, of a sales forecast, and of one or two things we needed to do, and if we did those two things, then we were going to be fine. The cash and the expenses would line up. We took the money with the understanding that it was going to take a little while for us to pay it back. If we executed on the plan that we had and cut our expenses as low as we could, we would be okay. If the things we focused on did well, we would be able to turn the corner and make the restart. And we did.

Every time ListenTrust has been in a restart, we've learned something new so that the next time we're prepared, and we don't find ourselves in the same situation over and over. With the flower company, we were too attached to the account. We were blinded by the opportunity it presented to open a center in Belize, and we let our egos get in the way. At the end of the day, they weren't a good fit, and we shouldn't have taken on their business. We could've avoided the entire situation if we'd been true to who we were and recognized that the client was a bad fit. When they first stopped paying us that should've been a sign for us to say, "Hey, this is not feeling good. As good as we think this opportunity is, maybe it's just a Trojan horse."

When we look at opportunities now, we are more cautious. If we're scaling a large business opportunity with a new client that we don't have a relationship with, we make sure we have leverage. If we're scaling business based on one client, we have to make sure there's a couple of hooks in that client so that leaving is difficult for them. We won't build a business division based on one client or scale too long with that one client because they take up all our resources. If it doesn't feel good, it's okay to get out. Not everyone is a good fit, and that's fine.

THE ART OF NEGOTIATING

Everything in business is a constant negotiation. Whether it's with vendors or clients, you will always be negotiating your pay or what you pay.

Often, negotiation starts with knowledge. To negotiate properly, you need to go into the negotiation with the understanding of the strategic relationship with the person or business you're negotiating with, and the leverage you have. Try to determine the value of your business in their portfolio and use that as a jumping-off point for your negotiation.

In a negotiation with one of our vendors, we knew we were their second-largest client and our revenue was important to them based on strategic things they were looking to do with the business. We understood why they wanted to bill in a certain way, and we knew what we were willing to give based on their billing cycle and our forecasted revenue. By entering the negotiation well-informed, we were able to work out a deal that helped our bottom line.

Sometimes we've had to walk away from deals to get what we wanted. We reached a point once where we had a client who kept asking for better and better pricing to the point where we were paying him for every phone call. At that point, we realized we needed outside help, and I contacted a friend.

My friend owns a global $100 million company and is quite successful. When I asked him for tips on negotiation, one of the things he said was that most Americans have no idea how to negotiate. Most people in other countries are brought up as traders because they're out on the streets hustling. They negotiate until someone walks away from the deal. "Even then," he said, "they don't come back and say, *okay, okay*." Often, they'll let you walk away and give you time to come back to them and accept your offer, or they'll give you time to present a new offer. If you don't present a new offer, they'll call you in a few days and say, "Okay, we'll take your last offer." In America, a lot of people feel like if they don't negotiate the deal, the deal is dead.

He recommended we go to all our vendors and negotiate to the point where they say they can't do it anymore, and then fire all of them. He said, "Go through and fire every single one of them, and see if they come back with better pricing." When they come back with a deal, say, "That doesn't work. We're going to look for other solutions. Thanks for your time. If you can come up with something better, give me a call, but I'm going to have to make a decision within the next week. Right now, you're not on the list."

I did the same thing with our clients. There was one person whom we gave a price to and when he said he couldn't do it, I said, "No problem. We'll help you transition." It hurt us to do it, but we told him we'd do a thirty-day ramp-down and move his calls to a new center.

A few days later, he called back and said, "Okay, we'll take your last deal."

I said, "The last deal is gone. When we redid the math,

we recognized we were paying you for calls. Here's the new deal."

He said, "No, I'm not going to accept that deal. I'm going to accept your last deal."

I said, "Sorry. You didn't accept it on the spot. That deal is gone."

He said, "Okay, then we're going to have to move my calls."

I said, "Yeah, I figured. When you said no to the better deal, I figured you wouldn't say yes to the other one. We'll keep the status quo. Let us know what we're doing to help you leave."

Two days later, he called back and said, "Okay, I'll take that deal."

Negotiating like this was a big eye-opening experience.

The best way to think about it is like buying a car. Usually, you go in, and you want to buy the car. They negotiate. You come to a price. Often, it's a little bit more than what you wanted to spend, so you should walk out. Don't get emotional or attached to the car, because there are a hundred different cars and there are better deals out there. Typically, when you walk out, the guy's going to come and say, "There's a better deal."

Walking away from a deal sometimes is a good thing. Leverage is also important. If you're calling somebody's bluff, you should call their bluff because you have a backup. When I'm negotiating deals, I like to know what's at stake. Do we want to stay with this client? Do we feel like they're gouging us, or do we feel, based on research, that the deal we negotiated a year ago is a fair deal? If it's not, then how do we negotiate to what is fair based on the research we've done in the past couple weeks as far as what we need and what else is out there right now?

If they're a good vendor or a good partner, I explain to them flat out, "This is what I need. This is why I need it. This is the reason why I believe this is a fair offer." If you've made the investment in the relationship over time, it's easier to go back and ask for a favor because you see each other as business partners.

When someone is a partner, you look at them as part of your portfolio. How do I keep them in there? How do I help their business grow? I want them to feel like they're attached to our business so when I do go back and ask, they know I'm not asking just to take money out of their pockets or cut their margins. I'm coming because I need it. I think it's a fair deal, and I'm asking for help.

When you're genuine with your needs, typically it's an easier negotiation. It might take a little bit of time back and forth, but you'll be able to shave some money off your existing contract or terms, which would free up some cash flow for you.

DON'T GIVE UP

A restart or turnaround is never your intention; sometimes it's just what happens. You can't avoid them, but you can learn from them and come out the other side stronger. No matter what occurs, my biggest piece of advice is to never give up.

ListenTrust has been through a lot of ups and downs. We've had more people tell us we're done than we've probably had people tell us we're going to succeed. But one thing remains solid: we don't give up. In fact, quitting is never an option.

When I think of restarts, I always have that image of the cartoon where the guy is digging for diamonds and finally gives up and walks away. But when you look at the image, you can see that the miner is just an inch away from the diamonds. If he'd just kept going, he'd have hit them. Every time we're challenged in any way, that's what I think about. I approach the restart with a "never quit attitude." I may be churning, fighting, and getting punched in the face, but I know if I keep fighting, I'll win. For every restart we've been in, we've managed to come out victorious by keeping that same attitude.

I never give up, and neither should you.

CONCLUSION

Asking questions makes you smarter. I know this firsthand because I never believed I knew it all. I still don't. When ListenTrust hits a brick wall or we find ourselves unable to meet payroll, we ask questions and we aren't afraid to ask for help. We seek answers wherever we can find them. Whether through a book, a conference, a chance meeting with an entrepreneur, or something else entirely, we believe the answer exists if we keep searching.

Over the years, I've learned that being humble and asking for help is a bigger strength than a weakness. It represents confidence in a personal ability to show that you're vulnerable and you're not afraid to grow. Be open to learning.

IT IS MORE THAN BUSINESS

Sometimes owners feel like they have to be at the helm all

the time. They believe if they're not working 100 percent of the time, then their employees will look down on them. They feel if they take time off for themselves and their families, then it might not be a good reflection within the company.

Always putting the business first is probably the worst thing you can do.

As a business owner, you should make a paycheck for yourself, but you should also make time for yourself instead of being so entrenched in the business. Don't just be the guy running the business. Get out and sharpen the saw. Remain interesting and interested. Have hobbies.

I've been around the block and around a lot of different types of people and businesses, and it makes me relevant and interesting. When I speak with somebody, I don't speak about what I do. I speak about who I am and what I like, and I ask a lot of questions of the other person.

If you relate on a human level, people will be curious. When you create relationships based on genuine interest as opposed to business needs, you break down the barrier of distrust. Don't be afraid to communicate who you are and what you want and need.

THINK BIGGER

We're in the people revolution. When you embrace that, you understand that core values and culture breed trust. Learn how to manage people and create dreams for your people to make your own dreams come true. How you treat your employees is exactly how your employees will treat you.

Be excited about growing people.

Don't be in it for the money. Be in it for the passion of what you're doing. Find your greater purpose while you're doing it. The money will be exciting for a while, but it's not what's going to drive you and the people in your company. Your greater vision and your company's purpose will guide you forward.

There have been times when my business partner and I have struggled to agree on everything, but at the end of the day, we both care about people more than we care about money. We both value relationships in our business. We may not be 100 percent aligned all the time, but our values are close. Our views on negotiation, integrity, and being true to ourselves and others are similar.

Culture begins at the top. If you want a dream culture, then cultivate a dream partnership.

Both personal relationships and businesses have cycles. Be sensitive to these ups and downs within the terms of the relationship with your business partner and the business. Don't get frustrated—instead, communicate. Be honest and open.

If you harbor your feelings or hold back your thoughts, you'll build resentment, and the relationship will eventually blow up. If you have a partner, you don't want to have somebody who's going to be a yes-man, who's going to mirror your personality. Find someone who complements you. Don't seek someone who has the same skills you have—that's a waste of money and a waste of a partner.

Find someone who does different things. Learn from each other's strengths and weaknesses.

Life is short. Partnerships are tough. If you can't look the other person in the eye when things are difficult and come to an agreement or talk things out, it's time to get out of the relationship. When there is no respect, the relationship isn't serving you, your partner, or the people who work for you.

This is the people revolution. Respect each other, respect your employees, work together to reach goals and dreams, and you will see incredible things begin to happen. That is delivering awesomeness.

ABOUT THE AUTHOR

CRAIG HANDLEY has never been afraid of clowns. He likes clowns. Craig will tell you that he is handsome, humble, and smart, and people generally agree that "Yes, he is a smart guy" and "No, winning second place in the beauty contest in Monopoly does not make you handsome."

He is an entrepreneur, which means so many things. He has done some speaking, teaching, and mentoring. He is a philanthropist, having given away close to $1 million in the last seven years.

He really views himself as an entertainer and musician who moonlights as CEO of his $13 million to $15 million company, ListenTrust, which was named #1 in Business Products and Services (#27 overall) on *Inc.* magazine's 500/5000 list, and employs over 1,000 really awesome people.

He believes in "living life like an extreme sport." As such, he has cage dived with great white sharks and rappelled down Table Mountain in South Africa, driven the Baja 500 trail in Mexico and hiked through the jungles of Malaysia, and in Iceland he snowmobiled across a live volcano, swam in the Blue Lagoon, and dove in the famed Silfra Fissure, which is the only dive site in the world where your dive is in the crack between two continental plates. He is the eighty-fifth civilian in the world ever to jump out of a plane from over 32,000 feet (HALO dive).

He is bold. He pretended to be security in San Francisco to meet Richard Branson and wrapped a twenty-dollar bill around his business card during the meeting. He's since been to Necker Island several times and has been kissed by the billionaire entrepreneur as a thank-you for the twenty dollars. He is a champion of all men, based on his undefeated record when donning the sumo suit in Richard's famous Beach Olympics.

He's met Ringo Starr and bumped into Paul McCartney before security escorted him back to his table while trying to get a selfie; and in Calgary, he had a scarf blessed while meeting the Dalai Lama (which he has since misplaced). He has partied with Akon, Snoop Dogg, and many other celebrities who asked him for his autograph (because they thought he starred in *Vikings* or *Game of Thrones* and he did not correct their thinking).

In over twenty years of doing business, he has learned that you cannot grow a business beyond your own personal growth. This mentality has caused him to invest in growth, to seek out mentors, and in general to search for growth opportunities as if he is a broken man in desperate need of fixing (which he very well may be).

He served five years in the US Army Infantry during the first Iraq war, leaving with an honorable discharge. Handley studied voice and piano in college. He has written and produced hundreds of songs, from rap to pop to ballads to humorous parodies, and has even opened for Coolio and hosted the Adult Entertainment Awards. In 2010, he turned down a record deal because it would have been "a pay cut" from his profitable businesses—and the required tour schedule didn't leave him enough time for his business or family.

He and his business partner are the founders of ListenTrust, a global award-winning organization in the call center industry. With over two decades of experience, they have been recognized by *Inc.* magazine's 500/5000 list and manage over a thousand employees in both the US and Mexico.